Makeup Optional

Lessons I Learned Working From Home

Lyn Conway

Makeup Optional
Lessons I Learned Working From Home

© 2007 by Lyn Conway

Published by:
A Fresh Perspective, Inc.
47 Asylum Road
Warren, RI 02885
877.441.6782

ISBN 978-0-9794539-0-8

Cover Design by Ad Graphics, Inc.

I Hope You Dance
Words and Music by Tia Sillers and Mark D. Sanders
Copyright © 2000 by Choice Is Tragic Music, Ensign Music LLC,
Universal Music Corp. and Soda Creek Songs
All Rights for Soda Creek Songs Controlled and Administered by
Universal Music Corp.
International Copyright Secured   All Rights Reserved

Printed in the United States of America

How to order:
See back of book for information about ordering additional copies.

Dedication

To Dan, Danny and Katie.
You have always been my WHY.
I love you!

This second printing is also dedicated to
the memory of my first recruit, Connie Gill.
Connie became my dear friend.
She was an "ace" and I miss her!

Acknowledgments

Many people helped me get this book from my heart and head to paper. This is my chance to thank them publicly.

First, huge thanks to my wonderful husband, Dan. He has been my rock for almost 40 years. Throughout this book, you will read about how he supported me at every twist and turn of my career. What you will not read is how he shopped for groceries, cooked, cleaned up and did the laundry while I was married to my keyboard for many months. Thank you, Dan!

I also want to thank my terrific kids, Danny and Katie. They have been my cheerleaders and fans every step of the way. Katie also read, critiqued and edited every page of this book, as did my sister, Julie Eilering, and my dear friends, Connie Gill and Patricia Brauner. They have all worked from home, so they provided a "reality check" as I wrote about the lessons I have learned. Plus, without their eagle-eyes, we would have a thousand mistakes. Thanks from the bottom of my heart.

A special word of thanks to all the women and men who have shared great ideas with me through the years. I have had very few original ideas in my career. Most of the things I teach, someone has shared with me. I thank each and every one of them.

Finally, thank you, God, for the enormous blessings you have always given me.

Preface

I wrote this book to help you be successful in your home-based business. Your success magnifies the success of every other home-based business person.

The lessons I learned and want to share with you come from my experience of more that 30 years in the direct sales profession. Running a direct sales business from home may appear deceptively simple, but it takes a high level of discipline to be successful. Some of the examples I use may not apply to you specifically. However, I believe that if you put the lesson in the context of your own business, you will find that you can relate it to what you do as well.

When you are persistent and consistent in your actions, you can't help but experience success!

Hugs,

Lyn

Table of Contents

Introduction

I'm going to tell you the end of the story first...I have had a wonderful career in direct sales. Being involved in this profession has blessed my life and the life of my family for more than 30 years. It's been an amazing journey. I've had so much fun and made so much money! I've made great friends – strong women who also took charge of their lives. My family and I traveled...remodeled our home...bought a boat...bought a bigger boat...paid for private college for our children...the list goes on and on. We did – and do – have it all!

You also need to know that the journey had some bumps in the road. For the first 15 years, I was an independent representative. I became a top seller and recruiter and I led a very large team. I joined not one, not two, but three companies that closed. Each time a company closed, my team looked to me to find a new "home" for them. When I got the notice about the third company, I was emotionally exhausted and decided to get out of the direct sales industry.

And I stayed out – for about six months. I missed it! I missed the fun, the friendships and the money. So when I was offered a position with a direct sales company as a trainer, I jumped at the opportunity! For seven years, I worked with Party Plan companies on the corporate side in Field Development. For most of that time, I still worked from home. However, from 1994-1997, I commuted to an office and worked "inside."

It was at the end of that four-year period that the name of this book came to me. I woke up before dawn one Friday morning. I had already put in a sixty-hour week. I never minded working hard. What I minded was putting on makeup before the sun rose, dressing in a suit and heels and going off to days filled with meetings. I thought, "I miss the days when going to work meant grabbing a cup of coffee and going to my desk...the days when makeup was optional!" And just a few months later, on October 1, 1997, I decided to start my own company – A Fresh Perspective, Inc. More about that later!

I was not a "natural" when I began my career in direct sales. I had no sales experience and I was incredibly shy. My success has always been a result of persistence and consistent actions. My story could be any woman's story. I've made a lot of mistakes along the way and I've learned a lot of lessons. Rod Stewart sings it best, "I wish – that – I knew what I know now – when I was younger..." Me too, Rod!

That's why my mission is to smooth the path for people who work in a home-based business; to help each entrepreneur achieve her personal vision of success. Whatever you want...whatever you dream of achieving...this profession can be the vehicle to help you create success on your own terms. If you are new to the industry or just thinking about joining a direct sales company and you are skeptical, please read on. I will share some of the lessons I've learned to help you on your journey.

Let me take you back...

I grew up during the 1950s and 60s in one of the "new" suburbs on the south side of Chicago. My Dad had his own business. He installed air-conditioning and heating systems. My Mom was...a mom. She cooked and cleaned and was always there when I came home from school.

I was a good student. My parents expected me to go to college. They grew up during the Great Depression and didn't have the opportunity to get a higher education. They wanted that for me, and I wanted it for myself. I have always loved to learn!

It was a time when career options for women were limited. Today, little girls are told from the time they are in pre-school that they can **do** anything, **be** anything! When I was in school, we were encouraged to become a nurse, a secretary, or a school teacher. My worst subject was typing, so I knew that becoming a secretary wasn't an option. I got sick at the sight of blood; so that ruled out nursing. By process of elimination, I said, "I'll teach!" Because I was very shy, I decided to teach really little children. I thought, "At least I'll be taller than they are!" I got my degree in Primary Education.

In those days, girls were less concerned about the BS or the BA after their name. What we really wanted was an "Mrs." before our name. However, we needed something to do until we found "the man." I found mine when I was a

Junior in college. We fell in love and got engaged, but my Dad said he wouldn't pay for the wedding unless I graduated from college first.

I got married two weeks after my college graduation. I started teaching second grade that fall and taught school for several years until I had our first child, Danny. When he was born, I decided...and felt I was expected...to stay home. It was the era of the Cleaver family. June Cleaver waltzed around in pumps and pearls. She greeted Ward when he came home from work with a warm kiss and a cool drink. The Cleaver family was happy because June made them happy. That was my image of a successful woman. So I stayed home. Our second child, Katie, was born three years later. By that time, we needed money and I needed a life!

When Katie was five weeks old, I was invited to a home party – my first. It was a daytime party at a neighbor's home. We were told we could bring our children. The hostess hired a babysitter to play with the toddlers. I sat in the back of the room on the floor and nursed my baby.

I watched the lady, Lenore, demonstrate various products. She wasn't very good, but people placed orders anyway. Not me – I didn't have any extra expendable income. After she totaled the orders, I overheard her tell the hostess that she had earned fifty dollars. Well, in 1975, $50 was a fortune! In fact, $50 was my grocery allowance for two weeks.

When doing my weekly shopping, I walked around the grocery store with a plastic clicker on my wrist. As I put something in the cart, I clicked in the price of the item in quarters, dimes and nickels. When I got to $25, I had to take something out if I wanted to put something else in. I loved to cook and I hated being limited to $25 a week. So when she said $50, I thought, "Unlimited grocery budget! I can do that!"

I hung around until all the other guests left. Then I asked Lenore if I could help her carry her boxes out to her car. She was an older lady (probably about the age I am now!), so she was grateful for the help. At curbside I asked, "Does your company have any jobs available?" She looked at me and she said, "Book six parties. When you have them booked call me and we'll issue you a kit." And she handed me a catalog with her name on it, got in her car and drove away. Who can blame her? I sat in the back of the room with a newborn, never said a word and didn't order anything. I'm sure she didn't have high hopes for me.

One of my best qualities has always been my determination. My Mom used to say to me, "When you want something, you are bound and determined to get it!" It was many years before I realized that she didn't mean that as a compliment! She was right about me. When I heard Lenore say that she had earned $50 in a couple of hours talking to adults, I was determined to have what she had. I know now that sheer determination is the reason that I was able to get started.

I went home and got six bookings. It wasn't easy, but I got them. I called Lenore and she invited me to the "mandatory" training meeting. After that training, the company issued me a kit.

I learned so many lessons during that first year in Party Plan. Eventually I became one of Lenore's "Aces," but it wasn't easy. And that's the first lesson I want to share with you.

You Can't Tell By Looking!

PART 1

Early Lessons

Early Lessons

You Can't Tell by Looking!

Lenore didn't know I'd be successful. **I didn't know I'd be successful.** I had no idea what I was getting myself into! I didn't even know I was starting a business. (I thought I was asking for a job.) I just knew that we needed some money and I wanted to stay home with our kids, but I also needed to get out and talk to adults once in a while.

Through my career, I've recruited hundreds of people. Some that I thought would be terrific did nothing. Others that I didn't think would do much took off and experienced success. When I signed them up, I probably guessed right about half the time.

I learned that I couldn't tell by looking, so the only way to find out if they had the drive and determination to be successful was to tell them what to do and see if they did it.

Lenore knew that I couldn't have a party plan business without bookings, so she told me what I needed to do. And I responded.

That's the second lesson...

The Power of Expectations

Expectations don't scare people away. In fact, people are calmer and more secure when they know what's expected of them. It's when they don't know what to do and nobody tells them that they're afraid. Lenore told me what she expected and waited to see what I would do.

What I did was get on the phone and ask the six people I was sure would say, "Yes" – the six people who loved me best – my Mom, my sister, my best friend – you know the people I'm talking about. When I asked those six people, every single one of them said, "No." Every single one! I was devastated…but determined, so I called all six back and said, "Someone is having parties. Who is inviting you to parties?" I got "referrals." (Later I would learn the importance of getting referrals. At that time, I was just acting on instinct.)

With sweaty palms, I called those referrals and got six bookings because that was what Lenore told me I had to do. Why didn't I quit after the first six "No" responses? Why did I brave the dreaded telephone? That's the next lesson…

You Need a Compelling "WHY"

With a compelling "WHY," you can move mountains! Without a compelling "WHY," fear overcomes you. Fear leads to procrastination. And if you procrastinate long enough, what you were thinking about doing doesn't seem like such a good idea anymore. No one does anything they're afraid of until the "WHY" is bigger than the fear.

18

I was really afraid and unsure, but I had a huge WHY. My compelling WHY was to stay home with Danny and Katie. Your WHY may be totally different. The lesson is to figure out what it is…and make sure it's big enough to give you the motivation to take action.

> *No one does anything they're afraid of until the "WHY" is bigger than the fear.*

I find that most of the time, the reasons WHY fall into five major categories. I call them the "5 P's." Most people get started for one or more of the "P's."

Product – They love the product! They want to purchase it at wholesale and they may want to share it with others.

Profit – Some want to make "BIG MONEY"…some just need a few hundred extra dollars a month to make ends meet. Either way, the money is important to them.

People – They crave people contact. They may feel isolated being at home with children, or are in a job with limited people contact, or perhaps they just moved to a new area and don't know anyone. They know that their business can be a vehicle for meeting people and making friends.

Purpose – Many people need and want something "more" in their life. More time with their children…more flexibility in their schedule…more options in their career path. A home-based business is their ticket to achieving an important purpose with a small investment.

Personal Growth – Smart people know that having your own business can be the vehicle to become a better version of yourself. Skill development and personal development are all welcome residuals of earning while you learn.

When I got started, I had four of the five P's. My most important reasons were to stay home with my children (Purpose) and to earn $50 a week (Profit). I also wanted to get out and speak in full sentences to adults on a regular basis (People). Plus, I knew that I would have to force myself to overcome my shyness (Personal Growth). The only P that I didn't have was the Product P. Lenore could have been selling dog food. When I heard her say, "$50," I was in!

No matter how compelling your WHY is, you have to find people who need your services. This is the lesson I wish someone had told me *before* I started…

Make a BIG List

I was sure I knew who would book from me. I was wrong, but I learned a valuable lesson. I learned how important it is to have a BIG list of prospects.

I encourage new people to write down everyone they know without prejudging, then assign each name on the list an A – B – or C. "A" people are the ones you are sure will say, "Yes." "B" people are the ones you're not sure of, but you think, "Maybe." "C" people are the "No way in the world…I only wrote them down because you told me to write down EVERYONE!"

Start by asking the "C" people…the people you think are the least likely to say "Yes." It may sound crazy, but when you approach the people you think are least likely to book first, you will get practice asking and some will say, "Yes" because they *want* what you have to offer. By the time you get to your "A" list, you won't be devastated if they say, "No."

The goal is to book into a number of different groups so you get to people you don't know. Nobody is successful in the direct sales profession until they get past the "friends and family" bookings and get to the public. In retrospect, it was probably a blessing that my "A" list said "No." It got me to the public faster and gave me the confidence that there were people out there who wanted what I had to offer. It also made me realize that the world didn't come to an end when someone said, "No."

> "Do one thing every day
> that scares you."
> ~Eleanor Roosevelt

When I started doing parties, I was sooooo bad! I got sick before every one. I did the parties sitting on the floor because my knees were shaking. At the end of the party, I packed the display products into two large cardboard boxes. During those early days, I had a recurring nightmare. I dreamt that the guests put me into the kit box, put a large chain and padlock around the box, and left me at curbside.

I was often in tears when I got home from a party. My husband, Dan, would say, "What's the matter, honey?" I would say, "I was just awful!" And he'd say, "Did you do *anything* right?" I would stop and I'd think and I'd tell him a couple of things I did right. And then he would say, "Great. Do that next time and add one thing more." (Dan was actually my first coach.)

Despite that excellent advice, I was struggling. Lenore knew I was struggling. She probably knew that I was close to quitting. She asked me the single most important question of my career. Because I answered that question, I stayed in the business.

She said to me, "How many times a week can you walk out the door to do a party?" I said, "I don't know." All I knew was I wanted $50 a week. She said, "You can't count on every party earning you $50. It doesn't work that way." She continued, "Talk to your husband. Decide when you can walk out that door." That suggestion led to the next lesson – perhaps the most important lesson I ever learned.

Treat Your Business Like a Business

One of the most attractive features of a home-based business is that the hours you work are flexible. Flexible…not optional. Your business can fit perfectly into your life. You just have to decide *when* it fits or you will "flex" yourself out of business.

Dan and I talked. We decided that three times a week was good for us – Tuesday and Thursday nights and Sunday afternoon. Dan was in school on Tuesday and Thursday nights and we had a good babysitter, so we decided that we would be out the same nights and home the same nights. That wouldn't be everyone's choice, but it worked for us.

The next time Lenore and I talked, she asked if Dan and I had decided how many times a week I would work. When I told her, "Three times," she said, "When?" I responded, "Tuesday night, Thursday night and Sunday afternoon." She said, "Are you booked every Tuesday night, Thursday night, Sunday afternoon?" I just laughed! But I was also angry. I was hardly booked at all and she knew it! She said, "You're going to work every Tuesday night, Thursday night and Sunday afternoon anyway." "But how can I work if I'm not booked?" I asked. She said, "Kiss your husband and the kids good-bye. Lock yourself up with a telephone and 'dial for dollars.'"

> "Nobody can go back and start a
> new beginning, but anyone can start
> today and make a new ending."
> ~Maria Robinson

So that's what I did. If it was a time I had blocked for work, I went to work. I kissed Dan and the kids just as if I were going to a party, I went upstairs to our bedroom, closed the door, sat on the edge of the bed (the telephone was on our night stand) and dialed. I did that for about three weeks and I filled my date book. I still have that first date book. It is my diary of the *real beginning* of my business. Every Tuesday, Thursday and Sunday either has the name of a Hostess or a list of names of people I contacted with notes: "Not interested!" "Call later." "Referred me to…" "Yes! Booked for…"

I remember one night in particular. I got booking after booking. It was so exciting! At 9:00 pm, I called Lenore to tell her my good news. She heard the excitement in my voice and said, "Keep calling!" I said, "Isn't it too late?" I'll never forget her response. "Lots of people are still up. When you're on a roll, don't quit."

For years, if I had a postponement or a rearrangement in my schedule and I had a Tuesday or Thursday night, or a Sunday afternoon free, I would still go upstairs and "dial for dollars." I knew I could get a booking in the next week to 10 days by getting on the telephone. That single piece of advice saved me, and saved my business.

Now, I can almost hear you saying to yourself, "That's fine for **you**, but I break out in a sweat when I *think* about picking up the telephone!" I know…I can relate. I was terribly "phonaphobic." I simply had to recover – and you can recover, too. That's the next lesson…

The Phone Is Your Friend!

Let me tell you a tale, my friends…

In the olden days, all telephones had cords. There were no cordless phones, speaker phones, cell phones or headsets. And you had to "dial." There were no push-button telephones. (This, of course, was in the dinosaur age.) The good news was that there were no answering machines or voice mail either. If the person you called was at home, they either answered or you got a busy signal. If they weren't at home, the telephone just rang and rang. It was a kinder, gentler time.

The telephone on the first floor of our home was a wall phone in the kitchen. It was mounted on a bulletin board with our family calendar. It intimidated me! The telephone is not a comfortable tool for a shy person. I could find a million excuses for NOT picking up the receiver…dishes to do, a diaper to change, just about anything was a good excuse. However, I knew that I had to stretch my comfort zone and get good on the phone if I was going to succeed. So I made a plan…

- I stuck a picture of my children – my WHY – next to the telephone.
- I bribed myself. I could have chocolate if I spent a full 15 minutes on the phone.
- I decided when I would begin calling and set the timer on the stove. When the timer went off, I was like one of Pavlov's dogs – I picked up the phone.

- If it was a time I had blocked for a party and I didn't have a party booked, I spent the *whole time* on the telephone.

Here's what I discovered:

- The first call is the hardest.
- Once you are on the phone, every call gets easier.
- It helps to have a script to *start* the conversation.*
- People are nice. They want to help you!
- You get referrals if you ask for them.

It took a while, but I recovered from my phonaphobia. Now I love the telephone! There is simply no better tool for connecting with friends and business acquaintances near and far.

> ## *The telephone is your most effective, least expensive business tool and you already own one...or more!*

I admit that it is harder to actually reach people than it was in the olden days. People have more telephones, but they answer them less. It doesn't mean they don't want to talk to you! It just means they're busy. So when you meet someone, ask them, "What's the best time and the best

---

* There are lots of conversation starters on my "Ring Up" Rewards CD.

number to reach you?" It saves a lot of telephone tag. You always have someone to call. There are people who like to be called after their kids are in bed. There are morning people who prefer to be called early. Some people with full-time jobs like to be called at work, or on their cell phone on the way home from work. You don't know unless you ask! When someone gives that information, they are inviting you to call.

So, I'm asking *you* the question Lenore asked me…"When are you going to work?" How often you choose to walk out the door to do a party depends on your **WHY**, on **what** you want to achieve and **how quickly** you want to achieve it. However, I'm going to tell you a little secret: no matter what your goals are, it's actually *easier* to walk out your door twice a week or more than once a week or less.

When you work regularly, you get good at it! You get comfortable. You enjoy yourself! You get a rhythm going. You're in the flow. You begin to feel like a professional. People begin to treat you like a professional. When you go a couple weeks between parties, you feel like a novice all over again. Every party feels like your *first* party.

> "You can work your business full-time
> or part-time, but not spare time…
> None of us has any spare time."
> ~Dr. Tom Barrett

I have worked with thousands of people through the years and rarely met anyone who couldn't identify at least two blocks of time a week to do parties. The great news is that those two blocks of time can be any time you want. You're the boss! One woman on my team was a single mom with a full-time job. She didn't have anyone to take care of her children in the evening; however, her mother was happy to take care of the kids on Saturday. Mona had a very successful business by booking two or three parties every Saturday.

That's the next great lesson...

It's Your Business – Work When You Want!

If you are going to have a successful party plan business, you have to learn to book parties! And the easiest place to book parties is at parties. You have a "captive audience!" The current hostess invited the guests and they came. They like you. They like your product. This shouldn't be hard, right?

I was a terrible booker in the beginning. I didn't get any bookings from my early parties. My problem was "technique." I'd look at a guest and say, "You don't want to have a party, do you?" Well, the answer to that is usually, "No." So I came home from almost every party frustrated.

One night, I was at a party and a guest said she would book. I was thrilled! (That meant one less time I would have to get on the telephone.) I opened my planner for her and she pointed to a Friday night. Dan and I had an agreement: I would work Tuesday, Thursday and Sunday

When will you work?

If you haven't already decided when you will work, do this exercise with me:

- Look at a calendar for an upcoming week.

- Pencil in your current priorities – the things you cannot or will not change. Do you... have a part-time or full-time job? Exercise? Go to church? Volunteer? Belong to a club or organization? What does life look like right now? Write it all in.

- Now look for two or more blocks of time that you are willing to commit to walking out your door to build your business. Pencil them in.

- Also look for a "pocket of time" – 15 minutes or more – that you can commit every day. These pockets of time are for business contacts and other income-generating activities.

- Make your business a priority. Show up for work when you have scheduled yourself and success will inevitably follow!

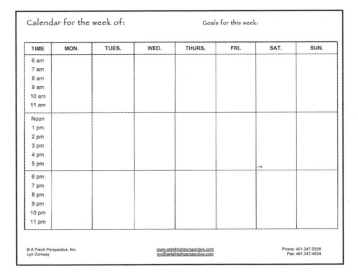

You will find a blank calendar and other tools on my website. They are complimentary. Go to www.getafreshperspective.com and print off what you need.

afternoon and Friday night would be "date night." It said "Date Night" right in my planner, but she ignored that and said, "Yes, that night will work for me." I was desperate for bookings, so I said, "Okay." As I drove home, I knew Dan would be upset. I was upset – at myself!

"How would the person I'd like to be do the things I'm about to do?"
~Jim Cathcart

At my next party, I thought, "There has to be a better way to ask." So I took a piece of notebook paper and wrote "OPEN DATES" on the top. I drew a line down the middle of the page. On top of the left column, I wrote "Day – Date" and over the right column, I wrote "Name – Phone Number." (Now, of course, it would read "Name – Phone Number – E-mail." Back then, e-mail hadn't been invented.) Down the left column, I wrote the next five dates that I was available. I put a star next to the dates that were within the next 10 days. On the bottom of the page, I wrote, "Book on a starred date and get an extra gift." At the last minute, I added a date and filled in my Mom's name, Yolanda Stevens, in the right column. I didn't want to hand the guests a completely blank Open Date Sheet.

When it was time to take orders, instead of asking, "You don't want to have a party, do you?" I handed the guest my piece of paper and said, "These are the dates I'm available.

How to use an Open Date Sheet:

- In the left column, write the first five or six days and dates you are available to work. You will add additional dates as you fill some of the dates on the sheet.

- Star the dates that are really close. (You can define "really close" any way you want. I used 10 days or less.) Offer a little incentive for someone to "book in close."

- If you are only available to work on specific days of the week, those are the only dates you will put on your Open Date Sheet. If you are available anytime, you have more flexibility in what you offer. For instance, you can offer Tuesday/Thursday/Saturday one week, Wednesday/Friday/Sunday the following week.

MY OPEN DATES

Day ~ Date	Name ~ phone ~ e-mail
★ Tuesday – April 17	
Thursday – April 19	Yolanda Stevens 484-4800
Thursday – April 26	
Sunday – April 29	
Tuesday – May 1	

Book on a "Star Date" and get an extra gift!

© A Fresh Perspective, Inc.   www.getafreshperspective.com   Phone: 401.247.0556
Lyn Conway   lyn@getafreshperspective.com   Fax: 401.247.4834

You will find a blank Open Date Sheet and other tools on my website. They are complimentary. Go to www.getafreshperspective.com and print off what you need.

If one of them looks good to you, just write your name and phone number next to the date." Then I went back to totaling her order. I got three bookings that night – two of them on star dates! I knew I was on to something! I also decided to put "Yolanda Stevens" on every fresh Open Date Sheet that I started. A little superstitious? Maybe…but it was my security blanket.

Your Open Date Sheet works because you position yourself as a professional and offer a choice rather than asking a "Yes" or "No" question. A choice also makes it easier for your guest – she doesn't have to think so hard!

If you are available to do daytime parties, say so! If you are available for office parties, say so! If you are available on the weekend, say so! For example, you might say, "I do daytime parties for moms who are at home with kids, evening parties and Sunday brunch parties. Which would work best for you?"

I've taught tens of thousands of people about using an Open Date Sheet through the years, and in the process, discovered some tips that make a good tool even better.

Tip #1
Put your Open Date Sheet on a clipboard and attach a mechanical pencil. (Pencil is less intimidating than pen.) If someone says, "I don't have my calendar with me," simply respond, "Don't worry. It's a pencil. The other end is an eraser. Just pencil in something that looks good and I'll call you tomorrow. If you need to change the date – no problem! At least this way, you'll have reserved a spot

on my calendar." It makes a spot on your calendar sound valuable, doesn't it?

Tip #2

Some people will ask to see a calendar. **Don't open your planner!** Your personal calendar is your business. (If it looks like the vast wasteland, they will wonder why you aren't booked. If it's really packed with entries – even if they are personal activities – they will wonder if you have time for them.) Instead, tape a small calendar for the next couple of months to the back of the clipboard and show them that.

Tip #3

Occasionally, someone will look at your Open Date Sheet and say, "Are these the only dates you have available?" This is code for "I want to book, but I'm not sure about the date." Respond by asking, "What are you looking for that you don't see?" They may want to book a date further out or on a different day of the week. If you are flexible, you can always choose to accommodate the request. If you can't, you can offer to find her a representative who will be able to do the party on the date she is requesting. (You will be surprised how many times the guest will find one of your open dates acceptable when they realize you are serious about sticking to your work schedule!)

Tip #4

Take an extra moment to ask, "What's the best time and number to reach you?" Also ask, "Do you check your e-mail regularly?" Make a note of her answers. The more information you have when you sit down to do follow-up, the less frustrated you will be!

One of the best testimonials I ever got about using an Open Date Sheet came from a lady named Allison who lives in New York. She came up to talk to me after an event at which I was a guest speaker and said, "Okay, I'm a convert!" I said, "A convert to what? Tell me more." Allison explained that she had resisted using the Open Date Sheet because she was worried that she would miss bookings if she limited the dates she was available. She decided to give it a try because her life was chaotic. She explained, "I work full time and have six children. I want to do 8-10 parties a month. The first time I offered the Open Date Sheet, I explained, 'I work Tuesday and Thursday night and an occasional Saturday. Here are the dates I'm available.' I was amazed! They said, 'Okay' and penciled in their names!

"The biggest benefit is what it has done for my family. My children know that Mom works Tuesday and Thursday night. If they need help with a school project, they know that they better not wait until Tuesday or Thursday to ask for it."

Allison continued. "Even for those reps whose lives aren't so crazy, using the Open Date Sheet enables the rep to be in control and that naturally conveys to the customer a sense of confidence. Customers respond to the Open Date Sheet because it lets them know they are dealing with a professional who takes her business seriously. Sounds crazy, doesn't it? That a little sheet of paper with lines on it can do all that?"

I gave Allison a big hug and thanked her for telling me her story. Allison is like many of the women I meet. They are balancing a part-time or full-time job and family commitments with building a home-based business. The women who do this successfully are the ones who are very clear about their priorities.

They understand the next lesson…

The Miracle of the 1440

Each of us is different in so many ways. Really, there is one way in which each and every one of us is the same: we all have exactly the same amount of time. I call it "The Miracle of the 1440." You have 1440 minutes in your day. Every one of us does. Nobody is blessed with more. Nobody is cursed with less. Occasionally you meet someone who seems to have 26 hours. You think, "She took two of mine! I know she did!" In reality, she is simply making smarter decisions about how she uses her time.

24 hours – 1440 minutes – and at the stroke of midnight that day is gone. I have heard "Time" referred to as "The New Currency." The analogy is very apt. Imagine that each day someone puts $1440 in your bank account. To keep it you have to spend it all by midnight. Anything that is still left at the close of the day will be withdrawn. Would you figure out a way every day to spend $1440? Of course you would! You'd make purchases, invest the money or give it to charity. You wouldn't give it back.

Your time is exactly the same. You've been given 1440 minutes and you have to spend it. How you spend it is up to you. But at the stroke of midnight, that day is gone.

Are you happy with how you choose to spend your time right now? Do you wish that you had more time to build your business? Here is the real question you need to ask yourself: "Is my business a priority to me?" We make time for our priorities.

> "Time is a created thing.
> To say, 'I don't have time,'
> is like saying, 'I don't want to.'"
> ~Lao-Tzu

Look back at the calendar you filled out on page 29. I asked you to fill in your current commitments – the priorities in your life that you cannot or will not change. Cannot or will not...change. Hmmmm. Are there some things you'd like to change? Are there things you said "Yes" to that you're no longer passionate about – or never were passionate about? Would you like to build your business with some of that time? Why not? It's your 1440 after all!

Lessons in taking control of your 1440:

- If you are spending time on something that is no longer a priority to you, give it up.
- If you are in the middle of a commitment you made previously (like serving on a committee), finish your term and then say "No" to the commitment next time.
- If you are asked to participate in something that isn't a priority for you, refuse gracefully.

I learned the last lesson from one of those "26-hour women." I had been asked to chair a fund-raising committee at my daughter's Junior High. I called Barbara to ask her to be on the committee. She said, "Oh, I would love to be able to do that." I started to get excited. Then she continued, "However, I simply couldn't do it justice right now. So I'm going to need to have you ask somebody else." "Wow!" I thought to myself, "I wished I had said that when they asked me to be the chair of the committee!" Barbara taught me to say "No" gracefully.

It feels great to choose how you spend your time! It feels great to have a full calendar of bookings. You feel powerful and you open the door to wonderful rewards...

The Rewards of Consistency

I carved out time every week for my business. I "showed up" for work when I said I would. I treated my business like a job and decided to be the best employee I could be. I started to improve. And I was earning a lot more than $50 a week! In fact, I earned more money my first full year in direct sales than I had teaching school – and I was a tenured teacher in a public school system.

As my skill and confidence grew, so did my sales, and I began being recognized for my efforts. Here's what happened...

The company that I joined had weekly Monday morning meetings. Everyone who sold anything during the previous week stood for the "Count Down." When they reached your sales number, you sat down. One Monday, I was the last one standing! I was the top in sales!

Now I always thought that I didn't need or even like recognition. I had never been the best at anything. I hadn't been prom queen, star of the school play or teacher of the year, and we all know moms get very little applause for cleaning house and raising children. So this was a new experience for me and I loved it!

They told me to come to the front of the room. I was all the way in the back and I felt light-headed as I walked up. When I got up there, everybody applauded for me and they gave me a ribbon. I said to myself, "I LOVE THIS!" They say that "behavior that gets rewarded gets repeated," so I vowed to repeat the experience as often as possible.

A couple of years later, I was crowned the "Queen of Rubbermaid" at the annual convention! They played the theme song from the Miss America pageant and sang to

me: "Here she is, Mrs. Rubbermaid." It was phenomenal! And I realized that if I could be "Queen of Sales" by working consistently just three times a week, everything was possible for me!

At one of those weekly meetings, I found a friend who taught me another important lesson...

Find a "Pacing Partner"

Picture this...they turn the lights off in the meeting room and turn on a movie projector – the old-fashioned kind with the film on a big reel. The black-and-white movie was about a qualification heat for the 200M race in one of the Summer Olympics. It showed the runners preparing for the race: stretching and running practice laps. It talked about their commitment and focus. (The comparisons to what we were supposed to do for our business were *inescapable*.) Then the starter gun went off and the race began. As the runners approached the finish line, two of them were dead even. The winner stretched forward at the finish line and won by a nose!

The person sitting right behind me in that meeting was Lucia Gruszka. Most weeks, either Lucia or I would be #1 in sales. Lucia tapped me on the shoulder and whispered, "That's why you're usually #1 – you have a longer nose!" I laughed out loud...I do have a longer nose.

Through the years, Lucia and I became the best of friends, but we began as "Pacing Partners." We genuinely appreciated each other and shared ideas freely. We were "healthy competitors," and the competition made us both stretch a little more to be our best. Lucia and I were not in the same company lineage, but we cared about each other's success. We encouraged each other and cheered for each other. We lifted each other up when one of us was down.

When the company that we were with closed in 1981, Lucia's son was in the hospital. He had broken his leg in a sledding accident and Lucia was spending a lot of time at the hospital. I did the research to find a new home for my team. When I found a company that sounded promising, I called Lucia and asked her if she wanted to come with me to meet the VP of Marketing. She said, "Yes." We liked what we saw and both of us joined that company. Neither of us tried to sign up the other – we were happy to remain "Pacing Partners." Our friendship is stronger than ever today. In fact, it has outlasted any of the companies we joined!

I strongly recommend that you find a Pacing Partner. Find someone who has a similar commitment level to yours. You can challenge each other to be the best that you can be. The going is not always easy in your own business, and having a caring, understanding peer will help you get through the tough times.

Speaking of tough times, that brings me to the next lesson…

Where There's a Will, There's a Way

There are always reasons *not* to work. No babysitter, sick children, an unsupportive partner, a husband that travels during the week, a move cross-country…the list goes on. Everyone has obstacles and sometimes life throws you a curve ball! The people who are successful in a home-based business are the problem solvers.

"Do not let what you cannot do interfere with what you can do."
~John Wooden

I had two pre-school children and no child-care during the day. The company I was with had daytime meetings and we were not allowed to bring our children. I had to get creative. I belonged to a morning Bible Study group with seven other women. We all had young children. One morning, I asked them if they would be interested in going out during the day without their children occasionally. All seven said, "Yes!"

I suggested that we start a baby-sitting co-op and care for each other's children. We set it up very simply: we used Monopoly money and each mom got $2000. Each child you left with another mom cost you $100 an hour. If I left Danny and Katie with one of the co-op moms for 3 hours, it cost me $600 (of Monopoly money!). I got money back by caring for another mom's children while she was out guilt-free! That baby-sitting co-op lasted until all of our children were in school and I never missed a daytime meeting or event.

Through the years, I have met many women who had challenging life situations – situations which could have prevented them from building a home-based business. These women are all problem solvers. I'm proud to share some of their stories:

> My friend SueAnn's husband worked out-of-town Monday through Friday every week. She wanted to do weeknight parties. She had a standing arrangement with a high school girl to baby sit every Tuesday, Wednesday and Thursday evening. She

paid her sitter whether she had a party or not. As you can imagine, she worked very hard to make sure she had a party every Tuesday, Wednesday and Thursday!

Joan had been unsuccessful in another party plan. When I asked her to join my team, she said, "My husband would kill me!" I suggested that she make a deal with her husband: he would give her three months to build her business. During that time, he wouldn't criticize or be purposely difficult. If, at the end of that three months, she hadn't proved that she could earn the money the family needed, she would quit and get "a real job." Joan and I made an action plan and she went to work. At the end of three months, her business was flying.

Oh, and that's another lesson I learned…

Success Builds Support!

Dan was always supportive. I was very lucky. Many of the women who joined my team had unsupportive husbands. I learned very quickly that nothing gets a husband's attention faster than a good paycheck! The women on my team who constantly complained about how hard they were working, when in fact they were hardly working, rarely got support from their husbands. The women who made a plan and worked their plan earned money…contest prizes…trips…and the support of their husband.

So here's an idea…tell your husband the "good stuff" that's happening in your business. Men are basically "fixers," so if you tell them that you are miserable, most men respond, "Quit that stupid job if you're so unhappy." (It's a good thing that Dan didn't react that way. I probably *would* have quit.) Find something positive and share that. And be assured, when the check gets big enough, you will have plenty of support.

Which prompts me to tell you another lesson…

Fake It 'Til You Make It!

You probably won't be very good in the beginning. That's okay – most people aren't. You'll improve with practice. One of the best ways to improve is to act like the person you want to be when you get good at it. Challenge yourself. Dare yourself to do the things you fear most. After awhile, you stretch your comfort zone and your actions begin to feel natural. They become part of the "real you."

When I was in 8th grade, my parents decided to send me to an excellent private high school several miles from our home. The high school near our house wasn't noted for academic excellence, so my parents didn't want me to go there. No one else from my elementary school was enrolled in my new school. I had to start making friends all over again, and I was painfully shy.

The school bus for my new school didn't service our neighborhood, so I had to take two municipal busses each way every day. I shared that bus ride with the same people and the same bus driver almost every day. I would watch people get off and say good-bye to the bus driver. Doesn't seem like a big deal to you, does it? But it was more than I could do at that point to say "Good-bye, I'll see you tomorrow."

My stop was the end of the line. I was the very last person off the bus on the way home from school. One day I said to myself, "Okay, today I'm going to say good-bye to the bus driver." So I went up to the front and I said, "Good-bye, I'll see you tomorrow." He looked over at me and said, "Good-bye." It was not a breakthrough moment for him, believe me. But for me, it was the start of something BIG! I realized if I could do that, I could do other things too. And so I worked on stretching my comfort zone, one step at a time, putting on a brave front until I felt brave.

Another breakthrough came my first day as a teacher at Teacher Orientation. I was sitting next to another first-year teacher who looked as scared as I felt. I decided to stretch a little. I introduced myself and asked her about herself. I found out where Janet lived and where she had gone to school. We got to know each other and often had lunch together during the school year. We became friends.

At the Teacher Appreciation Luncheon at the end of the year, Janet thanked me. I said, "For what?" She shared with me that I had "saved her life" that first day by being so outgoing. Me…outgoing! She said, "I was so afraid that I was thinking of bolting out the door. When you talked to me, I calmed down a little." I admitted that I had been as

About that Comfort Zone...

The dictionary defines it as "the set of physical or psychological circumstances in which somebody feels most at ease and free from discomfort or stress."

We like to be in our comfort zone. It's...comfortable. However, there is no growth in our comfort zone. We have to stretch it to grow. It's just like our mind. When we stretch our mind with a new idea, it never reverts to its original size. It's the same thing with our comfort zone.

People talk about breaking out of their comfort zone. That's a very harsh image. When I hear that, I picture my comfort zone being surrounded by a brick wall. And to move out of my comfort zone, I have to break down the wall. I want to offer you a gentler image. Picture your comfort zone as being surrounded by elastic – not brick.

Have you ever been pregnant...or know someone who was? When you first get a little tummy you're so proud, especially the first time you're pregnant. You want everybody to know you're pregnant! You wear that favorite pair of maternity pants for months. After you deliver the baby, you put the maternity clothes away. When you're pregnant the next time, you pull on that favorite pair of pants. When you put them on, they fall right down to your ankles. You stretched out that elastic!

Think of your comfort zone the same way. Every time you do something that challenges you just a little, you stretch out that elastic! And as you stretch it out, it gets bigger...and bigger...and bigger. Pretty soon, so much more fits inside your comfort zone. And you can be proud of yourself, because you've made room for so much more enjoyment and reward in your life!

afraid as she was. She said, "I never knew it." I never forgot the lesson I learned that day: when you focus on the other person and not your own fears, you open doors for both of you.

PART 2

You Can Have It All

You Can Have It All

How did you react when you read that sentence? Do you *believe* that you can have it all? Do you believe that your home-based business gives you the platform you need to create the lifestyle of your dreams?

If you haven't experienced the rewards of your home-based business yet, you may be feeling doubtful. Perhaps you know some successful people, but you're not one of them – yet. If you're not sure what it takes to be successful, this part of the book will tell you exactly what to do next. If you are already loving your business, this part will help you stay on track.

I didn't know what to expect when I got started, and I certainly didn't know that I had found a new profession. In fact, for the first few years, I thought that I would go back to teaching when my children started school. My Mom often asked, "When do you think you'll use that degree in education again?" (I know she was happy that I was able to stay home with Danny and Katie, but she probably wondered why she and my Dad had spent all that money sending me to college.)

Through the "middle years" of my business, I learned valuable lessons about building a business that endures the test of time. Stay with me...I will teach you the things I am certain about...

Believe – Choose – Act

Conventional wisdom would assert that the three keys to building a successful party plan business are to "book, sell and recruit." Somewhere along the way, I figured out that to develop those skills, the **real** keys are to believe, choose and act.

BELIEVE

Believe in yourself. Believe in other people. Believe in your company. Believe in your product or service. Believe in your ability to create the lifestyle of your dreams.

CHOOSE

Choose to spend time building your business. Choose how much time you will spend. Choose how you will spend that time. Choose to share your services. Choose to create your lifestyle.

ACT

Nothing happens without action. Once you have chosen *what* you will do and *when* you will do it, you have to get into action. The actions don't have to be perfect...or perfectly consistent, but nothing happens until you act.

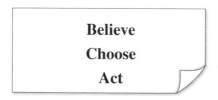

Believe

Choose

Act

I certainly didn't have the *belief* when I got started in 1975 that I have now. I didn't know about...

the friendships I'd make.

the money I'd earn.

the trips my family and I would take.

the personal development and skill development I would experience.

the many other women I would help achieve their dreams.

the positive effect my home-based business would have on my children.

And I certainly didn't know that the direct sales industry has created **more women millionaires** than any other industry on the face of the earth. (And some of them work 25 hours a week!) I just *chose* to get to work and to work consistently.

I remember the exact day my belief really started to grow. We lived across the street from a park. Danny, Katie and I spent a lot of time there. My kids played with other neighborhood kids and the other moms and I chatted.

One Friday, we left the park about 4:30 pm so that I could start dinner. We climbed the front steps of the porch and I grabbed the mail. The company I worked for at that time sent a weekly commission check. It always arrived on Friday. I ripped open the envelope and saw that the check for that week was over $1000. (In those days, that was a fortune!)

I remember thinking, "This must be a mistake. I didn't do anything to earn this money." I was at home with my children, I partied three times a week and I taught some other people to do what I was doing. Why would they send me this much money? All I was doing was working consistently and teaching other women to do the same thing.

Looking back at that experience, I figured out something that is truly amazing. With those keys – believe, choose, act – **the belief can precede or follow**. You can choose first. "This is what I want from my business. This is the life that I want." Then you can get to work and begin to see the results of your actions. As you see the impact that your choices are making on your life, on your family, and on other people, your belief will grow.

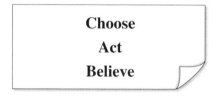

Choose

Act

Believe

Believe *me*, you can have it all. To get from where you are now to where you want to be, you have to know this next lesson…

Everything Is Hard Before It Is Easy

Think back to when you learned to drive, or when you learned to cook, or when you learned to play a sport. Were you really good at it right away? Think about anything you do well. Were you as good at it in the beginning as you are now? Probably not.

I have known so many people who gave up on their home-based business because they weren't very good in the beginning. Hardly anyone is! None of the individual business activities are complicated – talking to people, developing relationships, following up. It's not rocket science, but it's not easy to make yourself work when there are so many distractions working *from home*.

Plus, the learning curve is real. As you get good at what you do, it gets easier – and more fun – but it is hard at first. And you have to learn to live with "delayed gratification." What you do for your business today rarely has an immediate payoff. More often, you see the results of your efforts 30 – 60 – 90 days later.

Okay, now that I've dumped a bucket of cold water on you, let me offer you some encouragement…

Practice Makes Better

I'm sure you've heard the expression, "Practice Makes Perfect." I don't believe that, but I do believe "Practice Makes Better." And lots of practice makes you much, much better. When you practice the fundamentals of your business – booking, selling, recruiting – you get good at them. You develop a rhythm. You have fun. No matter how experienced you are, you still have to keep practicing the fundamentals.

"The minute you get away from fundamentals, the bottom can fall out."
~Michael Jordan

I lived in Chicago during the "glory years" of the Chicago Bulls. During the 1990s, the Bulls won six NBA championships. Many people believe that Michael Jordan was the catalyst for that extraordinary success. Michael Jordan is one of the greatest basketball players of all time. He possesses not only incredible athletic ability, but also an incredible work ethic.

During one of the championship seasons, Jordan's percentage from the free throw line dropped below his average. Legend has it that he went to the gym first thing in the morning and practiced. He stayed after the game and practiced. He practiced free throws until he got his rhythm back.

In his book, *I Can't Accept Not Trying,* Jordan says, "The minute you get away from fundamentals the bottom can fall out. Everything I did, everything I achieved, can be traced back to the way I approach the fundamentals and how I applied them to my abilities."

> *"It's not necessary to do extraordinary things to get extraordinary results."*
> *~Warren Buffet*

Practice your fundamentals until you get good at them. If you get out of sync, practice until you get your rhythm back. When you have your rhythm back, you will feel successful…you'll look successful…and you'll achieve extraordinary results. The extraordinary results don't happen because you do extraordinary things – they happen because you are consistent and persistent over time.

One of the challenges is that you are working in the same location where you eat and sleep and watch television. To do this successfully, you have to learn this next lesson…

Working From Home Is a Lifestyle Change

It's a lot like a weight loss program. To be successful, you have to view eating differently. You have to begin thinking about exercise differently. You understand that lasting results are not achieved overnight. They occur because you make lifestyle changes.

I found this out in my mid-thirties. In my teens, I could drop 10 pounds in two weeks just by living on hardboiled eggs. Then I got married and had two children. I put on 20 pounds and couldn't seem to get them off. I read a book that claimed the simplest way to take off weight and keep it off was to jog 20 minutes a day, so I started jogging.

Five days a week, I put on my gym shoes, did my runner's stretches and jogged for 20 minutes. People would ask, "How far do you run?" My response was, "I don't know. I run 10 minutes in one direction; then I run back."

I discovered that I loved to jog – and I started to see results. The weight came off slowly, but it came off and I felt great. And I looked great! (I recently found a picture of myself in a bathing suit that was taken about a year after I started jogging. I looked at the picture and said, "Who *is* that woman?")

I jogged for years until severe arthritis in my hips ended my jogging days for good. I had to find an alternative to jogging that suited my physical limitations. Eventually, I got new hips, discovered Pilates and incorporated it into my daily routine, and saw results again.

Working from home is a lot like that. The challenges are different from month to month and year to year, but you can always find a way to incorporate your business activities into your daily routine if you want to. And when you are consistent and persistent, you see the results.

Where do you find the inspiration to be persistent and consistent? That's the next lesson...

Know Your "Action Motivator"

An "action motivator" is a **really big WHY** that keeps you focused on working your business...a WHY that keeps you grounded in action...a WHY that helps you keep practicing the fundamentals. For instance, your WHY might be to earn enough money to get out of credit card debt. Your "action motivator" could be carrying around the Visa bill with the amount circled that you paid in interest. When it's time to get on the "dreaded" telephone, looking at that Visa bill motivates you to pick it up and make calls.

I learned this term from my friend Steve. Steve leads one of the largest organizations in his direct sales company.

However, he had a couple of unsuccessful experiences before he joined this company. Steve's father told him that he would never be successful in his own business. So Steve carried around a picture of his father. When he was tempted to play hooky when he had scheduled himself to work, he looked at the picture of his father. That helped him make the decision to keep working.

My action motivator was my children. I loved being at home with them when they were small. When they got into school, I found that I loved having them come home for lunch…going on field trips with them…being a room  mother…doing craft projects after school…all the things I wouldn't have been able to do if I worked a full-time job.

Doing things with them kept me focused on making sure I was successful in my home-based business so that I wouldn't have to go back to teaching school. Preschool, kindergarten, grade school, high school – I loved being home at every stage of their development and my business allowed me to do that.

What's your "action motivator?" Do you have a WHY that's big ENOUGH to keep you focused on your business? Identifying this single element can give you the strength to keep your business a priority and resist the unavoidable distractions of working from home.

Have you counted how many times I have used the words "consistent" and "persistent?" That's the next lesson...you have to be persistent and consistent ENOUGH.

ENOUGH

ENOUGH is one of the most important words in my vocabulary. You will be successful in your home-based business when you:

spend ENOUGH time on business-building activities.

talk to ENOUGH prospects.

book ENOUGH parties.

sell ENOUGH and recruit ENOUGH to make ENOUGH money.

When you do, you will feel successful ENOUGH to keep going.

If you haven't experienced the rewards yet, it's probably because you haven't given it ENOUGH time and ENOUGH energy. It's a simple business, but you have to persist long ENOUGH to experience the rewards.

I've worked with many people who love the **idea** of having a home-based business, but they have never gotten specific about what they actually want. They don't have a picture of what their business looks like. They haven't learned this next lesson. You have to...

Visualize the Business You Want

The brain works visually. My friend Jenny explains it this way: "If you are going to put together a 1000-piece puzzle, you better hope you still have the box so you can look at the picture." Until you have a picture of what you want your business to look like, your brain can't help you fit together the pieces.

Do you have a picture of what you want your business to look like:

> three months from now?
>
> six months from now?
>
> one year from now?
>
> three years from now?

Once you have a picture, your next step is to formulate goals so that you can make the pieces fit together. Your home-based business is a platform for creating any picture you want. You get to choose. Goals are how you articulate your choices.

If you haven't been very successful at setting and achieving goals in the past, this next lesson will help you…

Establish "Target Goals"

It may be difficult to imagine moving from where you are now to where you see yourself in your "big picture." Goals are the stepping stones. They help you focus on creating sections of the picture – one section at a time. Plus, when

59

you are focused on your goals, you *aren't* focused on the obstacles.

"Goals are dreams with deadlines." ~Diana Scharf Hunt

Goals keep you moving forward. When you achieve one goal – fill in one section of the picture – decide on the next goal right away. If you achieve a goal and don't set the next one, you are liable to take a deep breath, exhale and say, "There – I'm done."

Everyone knows that successful people are goal-setters. Yet many people don't set goals. Why do you think that is? Fear of failure? Fear of success?

Fear of success is usually a result of not knowing what that new place is going to look like. "What will happen if I actually achieve this goal – life will be different. Even if I'm miserable here, it could be worse there. I don't know!" That's why the picture is so important. You can keep imagining the place you are going...start living there in your dreams. As you get used to being there, the fear of success will evaporate.

Fear of failure results from making the goal "Win/Lose." "What if I don't make it? I'll feel like a fool. My friends will know I'm a loser. I'm better off not setting a goal at all." The best way to overcome that fear is to give yourself a range in which you can be successful – a "Target Goal."

Picture a target. You get points for hitting anywhere on the target. You get the most points for hitting the bull's-eye, but you still get points even if you hit the outermost ring.

Now apply that concept to goal-setting. The bull's-eye is your "heart's desire" goal…the most you can hope for. The outermost ring is your "no matter what" goal – you will settle for no less.

You can apply target goal-setting principles to any goal – business or personal. What do you want? When do you want it? The range can vary based on the amount of time you give yourself to achieve that goal or the size of the goal you want to achieve. Here are some examples:

"My class reunion is September 20. I am going to lose weight. My bull's-eye is 20 pounds. My 'no matter what' goal is 10 pounds."

"I'm getting married in 15 months. My fiancé and I have to pay for our own wedding. My 'heart's desire' goal is to have $20,000 saved for the wedding and a honeymoon to Hawaii. My outer ring is to save $14,000 to pay for the wedding."

"My company just announced an incentive trip to Aruba. I need to do three parties a week to earn the trip for two and the upgrade (bull's-eye). My outer ring is two parties a week because I am going to earn that trip 'no matter what!'"

"I want to quit my full-time job and stay home with my kids. My bull's-eye date is January 1st. If I'm not positive that my income from my home-based business will be sufficient by January 1st, my 'no matter what' date is June 15th when the kids get out of school."

The lesson here is that, with planning…

You Can Have Anything You Want!

My husband, Dan, took this picture of me on December 10, 2004 as we sailed aboard a 48-foot catamaran in Antigua, West Indies. The week-long sailing trip was my birthday gift to Dan. It was a week of sun, salt water, tropical breezes and magnificent food (that someone else prepared!). It was a week *without* cell phones or internet connection. It was a week that helped us both restore and rejuvenate.

As I sat on the bow of the boat racing through the wind, I thought of the entrepreneurs I work with. Most have the opportunity to *earn* spectacular trips from their company. *All* have the opportunity to *earn the money* to take their husband or their whole family on vacation, whether it's a sailing trip, a camping trip, or anything in between.

If you have a "regular job," your income is determined by someone else – your boss. If you have a home-based business, you **are** the boss. The only one who puts a cap on your income is you! Short of catastrophic occurrences, *you can have anything you want* with strategic planning and action.

> "Even if you're on the right
> track, you'll get run over
> if you just sit there."
> ~Will Rogers

If you're not used to thinking this way, let me teach you how. There are three steps:

1. Decide what you want and when you want it.
2. Do the math.
3. Work your plan.

Here's an example:

1. **Decide what you want and when you want it:** You want (need!) a new car right away. You've gone shopping and the car you want will cost $300 a month. You cut the picture of the car out of the brochure and put it on the refrigerator. (More about that in Part 5…right now, just trust me and do it!)

2. **Do the math:** $A \div B = C$. Divide the amount of money you need (A) by the amount you earn on an average sales event (B). This equals the number of additional sales events (C) you need to do per month. (I say "additional" because I assume you already have plans for the money you are currently earning.) Let's say you earn $100 for an average party: $300 \div $100 = 3$ additional parties per month. That's your outer ring goal.

3. **Work your plan:** Look at your calendar and find **4** additional dates you can work in the next month. (Yes, 4 – not 3. The car payment is your outer ring goal, so you need to insure against rearrangements.) Get on the phone and "dial for dollars" until you fill those dates. Go order that car! The first payment won't be due until **after** you've executed your plan next month.

What if you want to take a wonderful vacation? You need to create a long-range plan, but the same steps work:

1. **Decide what you want and when you want it:** The trip you want to take costs $3000 and you want to go in December – 11 months from now. You want all the money in the bank by November 1st. Cut out the picture of your destination and put it on the refrigerator.

2. **Do the math:** First, divide the amount of money by the number of months, i.e. $3000 \div 10$ months = $300 a month. Now, divide by the amount you earn

on an average sales event. Again, let's say you earn $100 for an average party: $300 ÷ $100 = 3 additional parties per month. A ÷ B = C.

3. **Work your plan:** Same as in the first example.

What if you choose to earn enough to get the new car **and** take the vacation? That's as simple as making your outer ring goal: "Hold six extra parties a month." All that's left is the doing.

> "You are the storyteller of your own life, and you can create your own legend or not."
> ~Isabel Allende

This is where a lot of people let the picture get blurry. Life happens. They get distracted. Time goes by. They don't have a contingency plan in place. They need to learn this next lesson...

Get Good at Plan B

You can't control everything, but you can be proactive about what you can control.

You can't control:

- The seasons and the weather;
- Events and circumstances beyond your influence;
- Other people's actions.

You can control:

- Your attitude;
- How prepared you are;
- How you use your time.

Things rarely go exactly the way we think they're going to go. All we can do is *expect* what we want and do our part to get it.

> "The most successful people are
> the ones who are good at plan B."
> ~James Yorke

My friend Lisa was on track to achieve her goal of leaving her full-time job by September 1st. Then her husband came home and declared that his company was relocating them half-way across the country. They would have to be there by June 1st.

At first, Lisa was really down. She thought she would have to get a full-time job while she built up her business in that new location. Then she changed her attitude. She decided to move her date *forward* rather than putting it off.

As she and her husband looked at homes to purchase, she told the realtors that she was bringing her business with her and she needed their help. When they chose a neighborhood, they visited the new schools that their children would be going to. She told the people she met that she was bringing her business with her and she needed their help. She and her husband visited churches. She told the people she met that she was bringing her business with her and she needed their help. She asked for referrals to doctors and dentists in the new area. When she visited the offices, she told the receptionists she was bringing her business with her and she needed their help.

By the time they moved to their new town, Lisa had a full calendar of bookings plus she had met people and become involved in her new community faster than she ever imagined possible…and she did not need to get a full-time job.

> "If you don't like something, change it. If you can't change it, change your attitude."
> ~Maya Angelou

Lisa chose her attitude and focused on what she could do rather than focusing on what was out of her control. There is a very important lesson there…

What You Focus on Increases

If you focus on your disappointment, it increases. If you focus on obstacles, they grow. If you focus on pain, you feel the hurt more intensely. Conversely, if you focus on the picture you have created of what you want from your business, you discover solutions you never imagined. Doors open up to you that you never even knew were there.

> *"You cannot depend on your eyes when your imagination is out of focus."*
> ~Mark Twain

My friend Vanessa made a wonderful observation. She had been doing yoga for about a year when she found a yoga tape for children. She loved yoga and wanted to share the experience with her two young daughters. She wrote: "During the exercises the narrator explains the 'tree' pose. (You stand on one foot while the other foot rests on the inside of your thigh.) As I struggled to hit the pose, the narrator said, 'If you are having problems balancing, find an object and focus on it. Focusing on an object will help you balance.' It was amazing how much that helped, but as soon as I lost focus on the object, I lost my balance." Vanessa continued, "Isn't that so much like our business? It is very easy to lose focus on your goal – especially long-term goals. Then you lose your balance. The good news is that you can get it back. You just find the object and refocus."

Find your object and refocus. My object was always my family, and the best lesson I ever learned came from my children…

You Can Have It All...Guilt-Free

The proudest moment in my whole career happened at my son's college graduation party. I had cooked for days getting everything ready. Pans of lasagna, salad and garlic bread and lots of desserts. I was carrying out a pan of lasagna as I walked by my son and heard him say, "No, I don't remember my Mom working when I was growing up." I almost dropped the lasagna! I did three parties a week, recruited consistently and led a very large team. How could he not remember me working? I went over to my daughter and I said, "Did you hear what Danny just said?" She said, "No." When I told her, she said, "I don't remember you working. We *always* came home for lunch. You were *always* on our field trips. You *always* sewed all the costumes for all of the school plays." None of it was true (except the part about sewing all the costumes). But that's what they remembered.

They remembered that I was there. They remembered the things we did together. Sure, *I remember* them tugging on my leg and saying, "Are you going to another party?" But they are not thinking about those times as they grow up. In fact, what I've discovered is that the children of successful home-based business women are more self-reliant, more independent and more entrepreneurial than any children I know.

So relax and enjoy the journey! Decide when you will work and work when you commit to work. Be persistent and consistent and you have a blueprint for building the life of your dreams!

> "One of the greatest feelings in life is the conviction that you have lived the life you wanted to live – with the rough and the smooth, the good and the bad – but yours, shaped by your own choices, and not someone else's."
> ~Michael Ignatieff

PART 3

Mind Your Business

Mind Your Business

Having your own business and working from home *is a journey*. It can be a joyful journey...or a stressful journey. A lot depends on how prepared you are. Compare it to taking a long car trip with your family. If you are prepared before you all pile in the car, you'll all have a more enjoyable trip. When you've done your research, know where you're going and what you want to see along the way, you'll feel in control. If everyone knows what time you're leaving, if you've got a full tank of gas, good maps, snacks and drinks, you'll avoid a lot of stress.

The lessons in this part of the book will help you prepare for your home-based business journey. Since the last thing I told you in Part 2 was to relax, the first lesson in this Part might sound like a contradiction...

Take Your Business Seriously

Let me explain. Whether you have a large business or a small business, whether you consider yourself full-time or part-time – it's *your own business*. If *you* don't take it seriously, why should anyone else?

Don't get me wrong...you'll still have a fun, flexible business you can enjoy, but you'll act like a professional. This isn't about how many hours a week you work. It's not about whether or not you have another job. It's not about how many children you have, or if you have a supportive husband, or if your friends approve of what you are doing. This is about you. Looking at *your* business *as a business*. Focusing your energy and your time on doing the daily things that show you are a professional.

> "The one important thing I have learned over the years is the difference between taking one's work seriously and taking one's self seriously. The first is imperative and the second disastrous."
> ~Margot Fonteyn

How does it feel when you say to yourself, "I'm a business woman. I'm a professional." Does it feel good? Or do you feel like a fraud? Perhaps you are saying to yourself, "I don't really act like a professional." Let's change that right now. Here is your first step…

DECLARE YOURSELF

When someone asks you, "What do you do?", how do you respond? If you've struggled to find an answer, try this: "I have my own business." Look in a mirror and say it: "I have my own business." The more you say it, the more natural it will feel.

If you ask someone who works in a job outside her home what she does, she will respond, "I'm an accountant," or "I'm an attorney," or…run through the alphabet of professions. They **know** what to say. YOU are among the chosen few. You are living the dream most people only fantasize about – you have *your own business*. Declare it with pride!

COMMUNICATE YOUR GOALS

Let the people you care about – the people who care about you – in on your goals. These are the people who will either be an asset or a liability as you are building your business.

Ask yourself a few important questions:

❑ Do my family and close friends know WHY my business is important to me?

❑ Do they know my work schedule – when my business is my top priority?

❑ Do they know when I'm NOT working – when they come first?

❑ Do they know how they can contribute to my success?

❑ Do they know what's in it for them to help me be successful?

If you can answer "Yes" to those questions, your family and close friends will be an asset. They will be your fan club. They will help you stay accountable.

If they *don't* know your goals and your plan, they can be among the biggest obstacles to your success. And who can blame them. If they get mixed messages from you, they don't know what you want or how to help you get it.

NEVER ASSUME

A year after I started my business, Dan and I left Danny and Katie with friends and went away for a Marriage Encounter weekend. Marriage Encounter is a retreat for married couples. It's time away from the "real world" – no meals to cook or children to care for. Dan and I had time to focus on us.

I went into that weekend feeling like I needed to be "Super Wife" and "Super Mom." Even though Dan had been completely supportive through the first year of my business, I *assumed* that he didn't want me to work. We hadn't talked about it; however, the little voice inside my head said, "Dan doesn't *really* want you to work, so make it all look easy! Make sure the house is perfect…the laundry is done… the meals are delicious and nutritious…blah, blah, blah, blah, blah."

Sometime during the weekend, I shared with Dan how I was feeling. He told me how proud he was of me and that he was happy to share the responsibility. He just wanted me to tell him what I needed him to do. Now there's a breakthrough concept – tell him – don't make him guess. I highly recommend it!

Something changed inside of me after that weekend. I was no longer afraid to ask for help…to admit that I couldn't do it all. Another amazing thing happened. It was no longer "my" business; it became "our" business – our family business. As Danny and Katie grew, they had responsibilities too. They learned to answer the phone "professionally" and take messages. They became world-class collators – stamping catalogs and making hostess packets. Katie sometimes came with me to parties when she got older. (Which is another reason I was so astonished that she didn't remember me working when she was growing up!)

CELEBRATE TOGETHER

And we all shared in the rewards. We made family goals together and celebrated achieving them together. One experience still stands out for all of us. When Danny was 11 and Katie was 8, we took a two-week family vacation to Hawaii. We paid for it with money from our business. When we landed in Maui and walked down the steps of the airplane, Katie threw her arms into the air and declared, "I'm eight years old and I've never been to Hawaii!" I hugged her and said, "I'm 35 and I've never been to Hawaii either!" What a joy that our business could provide such blessings for all of us.

The rewards we experienced didn't just "happen." They were the result of planning and making time for business-building activities at every stage of my family's development. Learning these time-effectiveness lessons is imperative for your long-term success...

Life in the Merge Lane

Imagine that you're driving down a limited-access highway in the merge lane. Cars are getting off at the exits and other cars are merging into your lane from the entrance ramps. That's how it is running your business from home. People coming, people going, distractions to blur your focus. The kids are in diapers, then suddenly they're off to preschool and kindergarten. Twelve years zip by and they're off to college.

No two days, weeks, months, or seasons are ever the same. Yet, your business can "fit" into every season of your life if you schedule it. Your calendar* is your map. By blocking personal time and business time, you control the calendar...you don't let it control you.

STRUCTURE GIVES YOU FLEXIBILITY

I love the *Seinfeld* episode in which Kramer painted over the lines dividing the lanes on the highway. He decided that the lane-dividers were too confining and that the drivers would have more room without them. The look of shock on his face when cars and trucks started crashing into each other was priceless.

That's exactly what happens if you don't establish a work schedule for your home-based business. Personal activities and business activities all begin to "crash into each other." There is no one to tell you when to work so you have to determine your "office hours." You may choose to work several hours a day or just a few hours each week. Whatever you choose, it's important to know **which hours**, because knowing when you *are working* also means you know when you are *not working*.

This is HUGE! I'm sure you don't *want* to work 24/7, and *none* of the people who care about you *want* you to work

---

* Monthly, weekly and daily planners are complimentary downloads at my website – www.getafreshperspective.com.

24/7. When people tell me they work *all the time*, I tell them, "No you don't." Thinking about working doesn't count. Worrying about working doesn't count. Working counts. So when you establish a work schedule, the structure actually gives you the flexibility you crave in your home-based business.

Look at your calendar and identify the blocks of time that you can commit to your business. If you have a family, involve them in this exercise. They will be much more supportive of the hours you work if they helped you choose them. Now decide how you will communicate your "office hours."

> **To your family:** write your work schedule on your family calendar. Be sure the calendar is hanging in a place where everyone can see it – like the refrigerator door.
>
> **To the rest of the world:** use the voicemail on your telephone to communicate your hours so that when someone leaves a message, she knows when she can expect you to return her call. You can change it every day if your hours vary from day to day.

My friend Janice lives in ski country and she loves to ski. When there is snow on the slopes, she is there as often as possible. I loved getting this voicemail message when I called her: "It's Tuesday, January 18th. I'll be leaving the office at noon today to go skiing with my children. I'll be back in my office tomorrow at 9:30. Please leave a message and I'll return your call first thing tomorrow." What a joyful, professional message. Anyone calling her knows she has a business and a life. They also don't expect a return phone call until the next day.

The signature line of your email is another great way to communicate your schedule. I loved seeing this message at the bottom of an email I received:

> Lori Jo
> Business Hours: 9:00 AM – 2:30 PM M-F
> Party Hours: 5:00 PM – 8:00 PM T-TH
> "I love what I do. You can do it too!"

Communicating your business hours is professional. Some people tell me that they are worried they will lose business if they are not *always* available. Professionals *aren't* always available. Have you ever called a doctor's office and gotten voicemail? The message will be something like, "Thank you for calling. The office is closed right now. Our office hours are Monday, Tuesday, Thursday and Friday from 9 – 4:30. Please leave us a message and we will return your call during office hours." Are you insulted that they don't answer the phone? Of course not! They are professionals – and so are **you**.

> *"Don't be fooled by the calendar. There are only as many days in a year as we make use of. One person gets a week's value out of a year while another person gets a full year's value out of a week."*
> ~Charles Richards

As your business grows, you will find yourself restructuring your schedule. That's fine! In fact, I suggest looking at your calendar regularly. Start by planning each month and work your way down to daily planning:

Monthly: Start with the "big picture." Take a blank calendar for next month and pencil in your priorities. What's special or unique about next month? Are there any holidays or vacation days? Is there anything that will take extra time? Write it in and check to see if the month requires any variation in your work schedule. For instance, if you will be on vacation for a week at the end of the month, you will probably want to schedule extra parties the beginning of the month so you still hit your sales goals for the month.

Weekly: Take time on Saturday or Sunday to plan the following week. Do you have any appointments or meetings that you need to note? Are there any fun events that you don't want to miss? When will you handle routine activities like grocery shopping? What business activities need to be scheduled before the week begins? What are your "office hours" for the week?

Daily: What are your top priorities for the day? What is your work schedule? Have you planned time for exercise and other personal needs? Have you built in some "flextime" to handle emergencies or other unforeseen things that come up?

> *"You = Your Calendar*
> *Calendars NEVER Lie"**
> *~Tom Peters*

Daily Planning

I learned an important lesson about daily planning at a seminar I attended in 1980. The presenter asked if we wrote down our top 10 things to do the next day at night before we went to bed. I shook my head, "No." I hadn't even thought about doing it!

She challenged us to start that night and do it for 21 days. She said, "It takes 21 days to form a new habit. Each night before you go to bed, write down the ten most important things that you need to do tomorrow – business and personal." She said we would rest better. Our subconscious would work on the list while we got a good night's sleep.

She was right (although I still kept a pad of paper next to my bed for those 3:00 am brainstorms). I got a restful night's sleep and woke up in the morning ready to tackle the day. I did it for 21 days and it became a habit. I made my to-do list that way for years.

Then, when I started teaching people to make five business-building contacts every day, I added a section on

---

* Used by permission of Tom Peters

Daily Planner

Day   Date

TOP 10 THINGS TO DO TODAY

1 _____

2 _____

3 _____

4 _____

5 _____

6 _____

7 _____

8 _____

9 _____

10 _____

7:00	_____
8:00	_____
9:00	_____
10:00	_____
11:00	_____
Noon	_____
1:00	_____
2:00	_____
3:00	_____
4:00	_____
5:00	_____
6:00	_____
7:00	_____
8:00	_____
9:00	_____
10:00	_____

CONTACTS FOR TODAY

Name, phone #, e-mail   Result

_____   _____

_____   _____

_____   _____

_____   _____

_____   _____

_____   _____

www.getafreshperspective.com
lyn@getafreshperspective.com

Phone: 401.247.0556
Fax: 401.247.4834

my *Daily Planner* called "Contacts for Today." My *Daily Planner* didn't change for years...until I read a book by Richard Koch – *Living the 80/20 Way.*

APPLY THE 80/20 RULE TO YOUR DAILY PLAN

I've always been fascinated by Pareto's Principle, also known as the 80/20 Rule. The rule states that "the great majority of results come from a small minority of causes or effort; that 80% of results come from just 20% of the causes." Pareto developed the theory in the late 1800s and it has stood the test of time:

Here are a few examples:

- 80% of the time, you cook 20% of your recipes.
- 80% of the donations at a church or synagogue come from 20% of the congregation.
- 20% of the clouds produce 80% of the rain.
- 20% of recorded music is listened to 80% of the time.
- 80% of sales come from 20% of the customers.
- And the list goes on and on!

Even so, I never thought of applying Pareto's Principle – the 80/20 Rule – to my "to-do" list until I read Koch's book. The realization that 80% of the satisfaction and stress-relief in my day would result from 20% of my efforts changed how I looked at my "to-do" list. I decided to give it a try.

I still wrote out the 10 most important things I needed to do the next day before I went to bed. But when I got up in the morning, I took a fresh look at the list and circled the two most important items on the list. Sometimes they were personal items – "make an appointment for a physical" or "pay the electric bill." Sometimes they were business items – "call to confirm the speaking engagement for September" or "get the new Tele-course schedule on the website."

TRUST YOUR GUT

Here's the interesting thing…when I looked at the list, I **knew** the two most important things to do. Often, they were things I had been putting off for awhile, but I knew in my gut what they were. Every morning for 21 days I got up, looked at my list, circled the two most important tasks and *did them first*. Sometimes they actually only took 10 minutes, but if I hadn't done them first, I would have been worrying about doing them – consciously or subconsciously – all day. I was sold on the technique.

I taught the system to my daughter Kate. I work from home, but she works in a corporate sales position. I said, "Try it, Kate. See what happens for you." She started doing it too. She called me and said, "This is the best thing ever." She said she had put off for days making a simple phone call to a client that she suspected was upset with her. She continued, "I made the phone call first thing this morning. The person was not nearly as upset as I thought he was going to be. When I explained why I hadn't gotten back to him, he was very understanding. I feel so relieved that I have been flying through the rest of the things on my list."

> *"Begin somewhere. You cannot build a reputation on what you intend to do."*
> ~Liz Smith

I shared this idea with a man who works in a large corporate office. He said, "Lyn, I don't even put things on my to-do list unless they're an 'A' priority!" I said, "Well, everything cannot be on the top line. On that 'A' list, there are some things that your gut tells you are more important than other things. Look at your list right now. Which are the two most important?" He said, "Okay, I know what they are." I said, "Call me at noon and tell me what happened." When we talked at noon, he said he flew through the top two, had such a feeling of relief that he was flying through the rest of the list.

Try it yourself. It won't take 21 days to see results. You will feel the satisfaction at the end of the first day and you'll sleep better that night. Over time, you'll also see an increase in your income. For example, if your "no matter what" goal is to hold eight parties next month and you only have four booked, you have to book four more parties. If it takes four phone calls or forty phone calls, those phone calls are "the most important thing" to do. When you make getting those bookings your top priority, you will see your commissions grow.

> "A major part of successful living
> lies in the ability to put first things
> first. Indeed, the reason most
> major goals are not achieved is
> that we spend our time doing
> second things first."
> ~Robert J. McKain

WHY DON'T WE DO THE MOST IMPORTANT THINGS FIRST?

We can always find an excuse for doing "second things first." I've used many excuses at one time or another, and here's what I've found:

I tell myself, "I work better under pressure."
This is the grandmother of all excuses. I used this one for a long time...until I realized how much additional stress and anxiety I was causing myself. Since I decided to change my attitude, I'm no longer losing sleep over deadlines.

I allow someone else's crisis to distract me from what I should be doing.
I'm a "rescuer." If someone has a crisis, my tendency is to bail them out – even though, long-term, that might not be in their best interest. When my children forgot their home-

work on the kitchen table, I responded to their phone calls by jumping in the car and driving to school. I did that until I realized that "forgetting" had become a habit and I was supporting the habit by my response. I have learned that the person with the crisis has the right to ask, and I have the right to choose my response.

I hate to let anyone down.
I usually find that I let someone down when I have over-committed myself. I've said, "Yes," to too many people and too many activities. What I've discovered is that I can say, "I'm sorry. I can't commit to that." Then if I find that I do have time, I can say "Yes" later and be a hero.

I look at the clutter and say,
"It will only take a few minutes to clear this up."
Clutter can reach epidemic proportions. And I have to admit, I like an orderly environment. What I have had to accept is that if I let the clutter grow, tackling it doesn't take a few minutes – it can take hours! So I have had to learn to put my blinders on and ignore it until *after* the two most important things are done.

I let the size of the job intimidate me.
I have learned that every big job can be broken down into many small tasks. When I start to feel overwhelmed, I break the project down into small tasks and figure out how long each task will take. Then I make a checklist so that I can feel a sense of accomplishment as I check off each accomplished task.

*"The space for what you
want is already filled with what
you settled for instead."*
~Richard Bach

TALK TO PEOPLE EVERY DAY

People contact needs to be high on your priority list every day. Once you stretch your comfort zone, you will find that people contact is the most enjoyable part of your business and it certainly makes you the most money. If you're really pressed for time, you can keep your finger on the pulse of your business with as little as 15 minutes of people-contact every day.

Try these tips for making daily contacts:

- Leave 15-30 minutes early for a party. Park down the street from your hostess's home and make calls from your cell phone.

- Schedule an appointment for the start of your work day. If you plan to work from 10 am to noon, schedule a phone appointment for 10 am so that your work day really begins.

- Always carry your prospect list with you. When you have a few minutes of waiting time, make phone calls.

Schedule a "Power Hour" once or twice a week. I've heard this term defined lots of different ways. I define it as a "self-contained hour." You have your list of people to call. You know what you want to say. You make your calls and you save 10-15 minutes at the end of the hour to keep any promises you made during the conversations. For instance, if you promised to send out a hostess packet, you address it and get it ready to go in the mail. If you promised to handle a return, you complete the paperwork. If you promised to call a referral, you initiate the contact. If you promised to send out business information, it is ready to go. Nothing is left undone at the end of the hour. There's a great amount of satisfaction in that!

TRUTH TIME

Even if you have a vision of success, in the end, it all comes down to execution. You have to actually spend ENOUGH time on the right activities to see positive results. For those people who are positive they are working all the time, I tell them, "Prove it. Keep a log."

A time log is a great way to find out how much you're *really* working. You only need to do it for a day or two. You will quickly discover whether you are working as much as you **think** you're working. Use a daily planner and log your activity all day. It's a real eye-opener.

When you look at your log after a day or two, you will discover your particular time-wasters. Pay attention to how much time you spent:

- Reading and answering email
- Surfing the web
- Watching television

- Digging through piles of papers on your desk
- Continuing phone conversations *after* you took care of business
- Procrastinating *before* you started the project
- Doing things you could/should have delegated

Unless you're aware of your time-wasters, you can't change them. Once you see them in black and white, you can begin to chip away at them. For instance, there's nothing inherently wrong with watching television, but you don't have to set your business schedule around the times of your favorite programs. There are all kinds of recording systems on the market that allow you to record your favorite programs so that you can watch them later (and even zip through the commercials!).

FIND THE SYSTEM THAT WORKS FOR YOU

You need an effective way to keep track of your appointments and your contacts with prospects. I'm a "paper and pencil" lady, but that may not be the best method for you. Experiment. If you are comfortable working on your computer, try using a program like Outlook or Entourage to manage your contacts and your calendar. Technology is changing (and getting smaller) all the time. You may find that an electronic device works best for you – just be sure to back up your files! If you like using paper and pencil, you may want to get a sophisticated planner like a *Day-Timer* system or you may just want to print off the daily/weekly/monthly calendars you need as you need them and use a binder or a file box to keep track of your prospects.

No matter what system you use – paper and pencil, electronic, card file – it only works if you get into the habit of using it.

Habits

> "Motivation is what gets
> you started. Habit is what
> keeps you going."
> ~ Jim Ryun

By definition, a habit is "an action or behavior pattern that is regular, repetitive, and often unconscious." It's simply something you do all the time without really thinking about it. Good habits have positive consequences. They help you stay productive and focused. Bad habits have negative consequences. They lock you into unproductive routines.

> "We are what we repeatedly do.
> Excellence, therefore, is not
> an act but a habit."
> ~Aristotle

A habit can be something you **do** or something you **think**. A habit is not an inherent part of your character or your personality. It's simply something you do *all the time*. Therefore, you can change it by doing something else or thinking something else in its place.

I remember when I had the habit of jogging every day, I imagined myself happily jogging when I was 80 years old. Then, when I started to experience pain after a jog, I skipped a day here and a day there. Pretty soon, *not* jogging was a habit.

> "Bad habits are like a comfortable bed, easy to get into, but hard to get out of."
> ~Anonymous

When you change a habit, you simply replace one routine with another. For example, if you have gotten in the habit of throwing your clothes on a chair when you get ready for bed at night, you have to commit to replacing that habit with another one. You can put a laundry basket next to the chair for any dirty clothes and take 30 seconds to hang up or fold and put away any clean clothes. Or, move the chair! Make a *conscious* effort to change the routine.

After you have done it with intention for 21 days, the new routine will become a habit – part of who you are and how you function in your day-to-day life for as long as you keep doing it.

Take a look at your habits. What habits do you have that help you to be successful? What do you do consistently that is holding you back?

If I can influence you to adopt only one business-building habit, it would be this…

MAKE FIVE BUSINESS-BUILDING CONTACTS A DAY

In my seminars, I teach business people that the most important habit they can develop is the habit of making at least five business-building contacts a day – a minimum of five days a week. You will be amazed at the difference this one habit makes in your business results.

> *"You cannot change your past,*
> *but by changing the small*
> *routines that make up your day,*
> *you will change your tomorrow."*
> *~Cathy Sexton*

Are you up for a challenge? Here's how it works:

Talk to five people a day about your business. It doesn't make any difference whether you talk to them on the phone or when you're out and about – just talk to five people a day. Voice mail doesn't count. Outbound email doesn't count. You have to **talk** to five individuals.

You're not responsible for the result of the contact. The challenge is to simply start five conversations a day. When you do that for 21 days, talking to people will become a habit. You will talk to 105 people, and you will get good at it. You will get comfortable with "warm chatting." You will get comfortable saying, "I'm a business woman. My company is (insert the name of your company). Have you heard of us?"

You may not get a lot of positive results during the first few days of the 21-day Challenge. A few people may tell you they need your services, but many will say, "No." That's okay. Frankly, if you're not hearing that word ENOUGH, you're not talking to ENOUGH people.

> "One-half of life is luck; the other half is discipline – and that's the important half, for without discipline you wouldn't know what to do with luck."
> ~Carl Zuckmeyer

I get lots of feedback from people who have taken the 21-day Challenge. My favorite email came from Lezli. Her email said, "I LOVE the 21-Day Challenge! It's like dating and getting married." I was curious, so I called her and said, "Okay Lezli…how is the 21-day Challenge like dating and getting married?" She said, "Well, when you're a single woman and you see a really cute guy, you think 'I wish I could walk up and talk to him.' You're afraid, and you dilly-dally and pretty soon he walks away. And you say to yourself, 'I REALLY wish I had talked to him.'"

Lezli continued, "When I moved to a new place, I decided I'd get involved in a dating service. I went on several 'first dates' a week. Sometime we just talked on the phone; sometimes we went out for a cup of coffee or dinner. I got good at starting conversations. One day, after doing that for a while, I saw a very cute guy in my parking garage. He was working on his Harley. I walked right up to him and I started a conversation. We talked for a while and he asked me out to dinner the next night. And one year later we were married!" She said "I never would have had the courage to walk up to him and start a conversation if I hadn't had the experience of going on lots of 'first dates.' The 21-Day Challenge is exactly like that. When you talk to people, you get good at it and they don't scare you anymore."

I challenge you – talk to five people a day for 21 days. I will be eager to hear your story!

Before we leave the topic of habits, let's talk about one other habit that can have a negative impact on your business productivity – the habit of doing everything yourself. This was a difficult, but valuable, lesson for me to learn!

"The beginning of a habit is
like an invisible thread, but
every time we repeat the
act we strengthen the strand,
add to it another filament,
until it becomes a great cable
and binds us irrevocably
thought and act."
~Orison Swett Marden

21-Day Prospecting Success Challenge!

DAY 1	DAY 2	DAY 3	DAY 4	DAY 5	DAY 6	DAY 7
1. 2. 3. 4. 5.	1. 2. 3. 4. 5.	1. 2. 3. 4. 5.	1. 2. 3. 4. 5.	1. 2. 3. 4. 5.	1. 2. 3. 4. 5.	1. 2. 3. 4. 5.
DAY 8	DAY 9	DAY 10	DAY 11	DAY 12	DAY 13	DAY 14
1. 2. 3. 4. 5.	1. 2. 3. 4. 5.	1. 2. 3. 4. 5.	1. 2. 3. 4. 5.	1. 2. 3. 4. 5.	1. 2. 3. 4. 5.	1. 2. 3. 4. 5.
DAY 15	DAY 16	DAY 17	DAY 18	DAY 19	DAY 20	DAY 21
1. 2. 3. 4. 5.	1. 2. 3. 4. 5.	1. 2. 3. 4. 5.	1. 2. 3. 4. 5.	1. 2. 3. 4. 5.	1. 2. 3. 4. 5.	1. 2. 3. 4. 5.

Focus on What You Do Best!

As my business grew, I found myself adding hours to my work week. I started to feel a little overwhelmed and considered alternatives. I asked myself, "What **don't** I have to do myself?" I like to cook. I like to work in the garden. I'm not crazy about cleaning house. I considered hiring someone to clean our house, but my Mom cleaned our house when I was growing up and my grandma cleaned her house. I come from a long tradition of women who cleaned their own houses.

I talked to my friend Lucia about it. Lucia likes to clean, so I thought she would tell me I was silly to even think about hiring help. Wrong! She said, "Do it. You'll help the whole economy." I said, "What do you mean?" She responded, "We're all part of the food-chain. You pay the cleaning lady and she can afford things that she couldn't afford before. And the people she buys from will have more money to spend, and on and on." Wow! I'd never considered that hiring a cleaning lady helped the whole economy.

I did it. She came every two weeks and it was great. The rule was that the house had to be straightened up before Morrie came, so once every two weeks, everything was neat and clean. You can do it too! The income from one extra party a month can pay for a lot of help around the house. Maybe you're like Lucia and you like to clean. Clean. What don't you like to do? Figure it out and pay to have it done, or barter for it, or delegate it.

> *If it doesn't take your unique talent or personality, don't spend time on it. Pay to have it done, barter for it or delegate it to someone else.*

Focus on what you do best. Do what you like to do. You will be more productive, have more energy and more fun.

LEARN TO DELEGATE

I just told you to delegate things you don't like to do, or that you're not good at, or that don't require your unique talent or personality. This was a hard lesson for me to learn because I like control. If I did "it" myself, I knew "it" would get done and be done right. Delegating meant I had to release control.

My friend Dolores is one of my mentors and a marvelous teacher. She put it in perspective for me. At a point in her career when tasks were beginning to overwhelm her, she asked for help from her husband. Among other things, he volunteered to do the laundry. One day, he discovered Dolores taking the towels out of the linen closet and refolding them. Her husband asked her why she was spending time refolding towels. She explained that she always folded the towels in thirds lengthwise, then in half, and then in half again. He responded, "There is more than one way to fold a towel, Dolores."

The lesson here is that when you trust someone enough to delegate to them, you can either teach them how you want "it" done or accept that "it" can be done well even if "it" is done differently. The important thing is that you don't have to do "it" anymore and that you can spend your time on things that **do** require your unique talent or personality.

Boundaries

You set the tone for how others treat you and your business. Communicating your goals, planning your time and acting on your plan, doing what you do best and delegating the rest...these are all ways to establish boundaries for yourself as a business person. You teach people how to treat you. Some people just learn more quickly than others.

My friend Mollye told me a great story about setting boundaries. Her sister-in-law lives on a small lake. Her lawn was constantly being invaded by geese – doing what geese do. She got tired of cleaning up the mess so she went to a hardware store and got a couple of wooden stakes and some string. She put the stakes at the back of her lawn on both sides of her lot about 10 feet up from the lake. She connected the stakes with the string about eight inches off the ground. When the geese came waddling up, even though they could have pushed past the string, they stayed on their part of the lawn and the rest became a "goose-free zone."

When Mollye told this story, someone asked her, "Did your sister-in-law need to leave the stakes and the string up or did the geese learn the lesson?" Mollye responded, "Geese have a very short attention span. My sister-in-law had to leave it up, or the geese would have been all over the lawn again."

Sometimes the people in our life have short attention spans. The boundary we establish doesn't have to be a wall that closes off communication. Rather, it can be flexible like the stakes and the string. We are merely identifying the space we need. We can "leave the stakes and the string up" and then move the boundaries as our needs change.

Boundaries are a good thing. When you establish boundaries and set expectations of how you want to be treated, people begin to look at you differently. They will treat you with respect and you will all enjoy the journey more.

> "It's important that people know what you stand for. It's equally important that they know what you won't stand for."
> ~Mary Waldrop

Set Up Your Office Space

It doesn't matter what you designate as your "office space." You may have the luxury of having a separate office or you may claim a corner of your living room. Either way, when you're in that space, you know you are "at work." You may decide to purchase a file cabinet or you may use a cardboard box. Either way, you have a place to put your paperwork so you can find it when you need it.

My first "office" was a card table next to the furnace in the basement. Our home was built in 1907, so you can probably imagine how dark and dingy it was. The space wasn't pretty, but it was functional. I had a telephone and a file cabinet, and I taped inspirational posters all over the cement block walls to liven it up. Now I have a beautiful office with lots of windows that allow me to look out into my garden. But I still have the same challenges keeping my office space functional. Organization is an ongoing challenge for me.

Get as Organized as You Need to Be

The goal of being organized is simply to be as productive as possible during the time you choose to spend working. You may need a very high level of organization or you may function very well with less visible order. The level of organization you need is unique to you. You need as much organization as it takes for you to get the greatest amount done in the smallest amount of time.

Here are some things to take into consideration...

YOUR WORKSPACE

My friend Kimberly Medlock is a professional organizer and a member of the National Association of Professional Organizers (NAPO). Kimberly teaches that most people are either an "innie" or an "outie." (Read on...it's not what you think!)

> **Innies:** Innies like a clean desktop. They file papers in file folders in a file cabinet. When they need a particular folder, they locate it easily, do what they need to do and return it to it's home – out of sight.

Outies: For an outie, out of sight is out of mind. Outies like to have their papers visible. At their most organized, they have their folders standing in desktop file racks or vertical organizers with the folder tabs clearly visible. At their least organized, they have piles of papers and folders on their desk.

I'm an outie. I *have* file cabinets, but the only papers I put in them are the things that I don't want to throw away because I may need them "someday." The paperwork that I need for my current projects is sitting out where I can see it.

Before I went in for my first hip-replacement surgery, the piles of paper in my office had gotten totally out of control. The tipping point came when I was spending more time looking for things than actually working. I needed to get everything organized before I went into surgery because my assistant was going to have to be able to find things while I was in the hospital and for a couple of weeks afterwards while I was recuperating.

It was a month before my surgery. I gave some thought to what kind of a system I wanted to use and I spent $20 on vertical organizers and colored file folders that could sit on top of my desk. I estimated that it would take two full days to clean my office. I didn't have two full days to devote to organization, so I got up an hour earlier every day. I set the timer for one hour and spent that hour going through papers. At the end of the hour, I started my "regular" work day. My bull's-eye was to be done in a week. My "no matter what" goal was to be finished before I went to the hospital.

Things got a lot worse before they got better. I had piles of papers and file folders labeled to hold the papers I wanted to keep. I also had bags and bags of paper to recycle. I finished in two weeks – two ahead of my "no-matter-what" goal. What a feeling of relief to know that I could say to my assistant, "That's in the green file folder in the vertical organizer to the left of the computer."

If you're in an organizational quandary, these lessons are worth learning:

- It may take some time to get organized, but it's worth it!
- Make a plan before you start ripping things apart.
- Invest in a few tools. They will help you keep organized afterwards.

When you mind your business, you will achieve what you planned. You'll stay on track and have a track-record of achieving your goals. You may even find you love your business so much that you want to share it with others.

> *"Most people never run far enough on their first wind to find out they've got a second. Give your dreams all you've got and you'll be amazed at the energy that comes out of you."*
> *~William James*

PART 4

Share What You Love

Share What You Love

Today, my passion is recruiting. I know that the most important service I can offer someone is the chance to choose a business that can change her life. I also know that recruiting is the only way to tap into that "residual income" for which the direct sales industry is famous. But I didn't always think that way. I began my business for *me* and for *my family*. Initially, it didn't even occur to me to offer my business opportunity to anyone else. If that's where you are right now, you may need to read this part of the book a couple of times because I'm going to share the lessons I learned about recruiting.

When I started to get good at sales, Lenore took me aside and said, "You should recruit." I asked, "Why?" She responded, "You'll earn more money." I was already earning **much** more money than I ever imagined I would earn. That particular company issued you a car when you promoted to Manager, so she said, "The company will provide a car for you." Dan and I had two cars, so that wasn't a motivator. She knew I loved recognition so she told me about the recognition for recruiting. I was already basking in recognition for my weekly sales. I didn't need more recognition. So she dropped the conversation and months went by.

I got my first recruit completely by accident. My Mom rented cottages in Michigan about 100 miles from our home in Oak Park, Illinois. She asked me to run an ad for renters in my local newspaper. One day the phone rang and it was a lady named Connie Gill inquiring about the ad. I described the cottages, told her what dates were available and she picked a week.

I needed to know how many people were going to be in the cottage, so I said, "Tell me about your family." She told me that she was married and had a four-year old daughter named Katie. I said, "That's *my* little girl's name."

She seemed like a nice lady, so I kept asking questions. I asked Connie if she worked. (Now, of course, it would be more politically correct to ask, "Do you work outside the home?", but it was 1976...I just said, "Do you work?") She said "Yes, I work part-time at Sears." I said, "That sounds like fun." She said, "Fun? No, not especially. But it's something to do." I asked, "Do you get to pick when you work?" She responded, "No, the part-timers don't get to pick when they work. They're assigned what the full-timers don't want." And I said, "Oh, that's got to be hard." And she said, "Yes, it's mostly weekends and holidays." And I said, "Well, I hope they pay you a lot." She said she netted about $50 working 20 hours a week. And out of my mouth popped, "Gosh – I make that in one night!" Connie said, "I'd sure like to know how."

Connie is one of my dearest friends to this day, and she claims I've never moved faster in my life. I packed up my two kids and the diaper bag, drove the four blocks to her home and was on her doorstep in about ten minutes.

We sat at her kitchen table and got to know each other. We talked about how my business could fit in her life – give her the flexibility to work when she wanted, work far fewer hours and earn much more money. Connie signed up on the spot and I had my first recruit.

Connie was **outstanding**. She consistently did three parties a week and was always one of the top salespeople in the company. Connie taught me several important lessons:

- You need a compelling WHY to recruit.
- Every recruit adds seven days to your week.
- Not every recruit is like Connie.

You Need a Compelling WHY to Recruit

Because of Connie, I discovered *my* reason for recruiting. My recruiting WHY was not the recognition, the car or the additional money. I began to recruit when I realized that it wasn't about **me**. I had something valuable and I wanted other people to share it.

In Part 1, I asked you to identify your compelling WHY for building your business – a WHY big enough to inspire you to take action and overcome obstacles. It's equally important to identify a compelling WHY to share your business with others. It may be the same as your WHY for booking parties and selling, or it may be different.

Take a fresh look at the 5 P's: Product, Profit, People, Purpose and Personal Growth. Recruiting can lead to

MORE of all these P's. Recruiting also generates a sixth "P." In fact, I don't believe you can be a successful recruiter without it. The sixth P is **Passion**. When you have Passion for your business, you **want** to share it with others.

Maybe you're like I was in the beginning – you simply haven't thought about recruiting. Or, you may be afraid to recruit. Fears are normal and can be dealt with.

What fears am I talking about?

- Fear of not knowing what to say
- Fear of not having all the answers
- Fear of being pushy
- Fear that it will take too much time
- Fear that they will say "No"
- Fear of losing business

"Fear is a darkroom
where negatives develop."
~Usman Asif

Let's address them one at a time:

Fear of not knowing what to say
It really doesn't make any difference *what* you say – as long as you care about the person you are talking to. As my friend Donna tells her team, "Say anything. Mumble something. Just keep the conversation going so she has time

to tell you what she needs." Recruiting isn't about having the right *words*…it's about having the right *attitude*.

Fear of not having all the answers

Here's a riddle for you: "How was the new consultant able to recruit her friend before she did her first party?" Answer: "Enthusiasm!" The IASM in enthusiasm stands for "I Am Sold Myself." New people share naturally because they are excited. They only stop sharing when they start worrying about "knowing enough." You can always bring the questions to your upline or call your company. That's why they're there.

Fear of being pushy

The definition of "pushy" is "excessively aggressive or forceful in dealing with others." Does that sound like you? Of course not! You are only in danger of being perceived as pushy if you are attempting to *convince* someone to join you against their will. (In my recruiting vocabulary, "convince" is a dirty word.) There is nothing pushy about offering someone the *opportunity to choose* something that will make her life better.

Fear that it will take too much time

It is true that recruiting does require an investment of time. It's a long-term investment. When you sell a product, you earn commission and recoup your time-investment quickly. The activity of recruiting doesn't provide an immediate return on your investment. Instead, you get your investment back with interest when the person you recruit builds a successful business and you earn override commission on their sales.

Fear that they will say "No"
It's curious how much power the word "No" has over us. It probably goes back to when we were two years old and tried to stick a paper clip into an outlet. Someone said "NO" to us in a stern voice.

Well, we're adults now. Let's diffuse the power in the word. People often say "No" by default. It's easier than dealing with the consequences of saying "Yes." And when they say "No," it usually indicates a need to "know," rather than a complete lack of interest.

Here are two things to keep in mind:

- We are not responsible for the answer. We are only responsible for giving someone the chance to choose.

- We get used to hearing "No" when we hear it enough times. Make a game of it. Use my "'No' is NO PROBLEM" sheet, and you'll be a pro at "No" by the time you're done!

Fear of losing business
Look at your hometown. Could you reach everyone who may want your services in the amount of time you have to do parties? Now draw a circle 20...30...40 miles around your home. Could you reach all those people on your own? Probably not.

But if you don't have a full booking calendar, this fear of losing some of your business to a new recruit will plague you. The best antidote is to get good at booking. Once I learned to book and knew that I could book in close using

"No" is NO PROBLEM!

If you ever feel discouraged when you hear the word "No,' remember that if you don't hear "No" ENOUGH, you're not asking ENOUGH people!

No	No	No	No	No	No	No Reward	No	No	No
No	No	No	No	No	No Reward	No	No	No	No
No	No	No	No Reward	No	No	No	No	No	No
No	No Reward	No	No	No	No	No	No Reward	No	No
No	No	No	No Reward	No	No	No	No	No	No
No Reward	No	No	No	No	No	No	No	No Reward	No
No	No	No	No Reward	No	No	No	No	No	No
No	No Reward	No	No	No	No	No	No	No Reward	No
No	No	No	No	No Reward	No	No	No	No	No
No	No	No Reward	No	No	No	No	No	No	No Reward

Reward yourself as you go along so you don't get discouraged. You choose the rewards! When you get to that "No," reward yourself with whatever you wrote in the square!

* To take the challenge, print off the "'No' is NO PROBLEM" sheet from my website – www.getafreshperspective.com.

my Open Date Sheet, the fear of losing business evaporated. My personal comfort level was to schedule three parties each week for the next four weeks. When my calendar was full, I didn't have to worry about recruiting a hostess. I knew I could give her the bookings from her party without putting my personal party schedule in jeopardy.

I can forget about myself and my fears of recruiting when I feel secure in my personal business. If you want to get good at recruiting, remember these letters...

FAYC

FAYC is an acronym for Forget About Yourself Completely. Recruiting is not *about* you – it's a selfless activity. Your fears about recruiting relate to what's going on in *your* head and heart. They ignore the other person...the person who might *need* your business opportunity...the person who's life could be changed for the better.

Your job is just to offer – you are not responsible for the response. Push your fears away because the *next* person to whom you offer the business opportunity could have a life-changing experience. To replace fear with confidence, use these simple strategies:

START WITH HEART

Start by forgetting about what recruiting is going to do for you. Think about what you will *give* the people that you meet, not what you will *get* from them. Believe in yourself! Believe that you are a generous person who offers from her heart.

Ask Everyone!

Be an "equal opportunity asker." It's so much easier than deciding who might be interested. Everyone has the right to make up her own mind.

Don't Care About the Outcome

I know that sounds crazy, but if you truly don't care whether she says "Yes" or "No," you will feel much more comfortable asking.

Be a Good Listener

People will tell you what they need if you spend more time listening than talking. The best recruiters are the best relationship builders. When you value the relationship more than the recruit, you will make it a satisfying experience for both of you.

> "Wisdom is the reward
> for a lifetime of listening...when
> you'd have preferred to talk."
> ~D.J. Kaufman

Keep Your Funnel Full

When you talk to *many* people about your business opportunity, the law of averages will guarantee that *some* of them will be interested. You aren't worried about any *particular* person saying, "Yes," and you never have to pressure anyone.

I like to visualize a funnel. Every time you talk to someone about your business, imagine the person dropping into your funnel. Some people aren't interested at all and they pop back out of the funnel right away. Some of the people in your funnel are **really** interested and they immediately drop to the bottom and come out as a new recruit. Others aren't interested right now, but you keep in touch and build a relationship with them. Each time you talk to them, they "gain a little weight" and drop lower in the funnel. When the timing is right for them, they come out the bottom of the funnel as a new recruit. The image of a funnel full of prospects helps me keep recruiting in perspective.

And here's some exciting news! While you are forgetting about yourself completely and sharing what you love, you are reaping the rewards of recruiting. That's the second lesson I learned from Connie...

Every New Recruit Adds Seven Days to Your Week

Even if you decided that you were going to hold parties every day of the week, there's a physical limit to how many parties you can do. When you recruit, you:

Expand your reach

Now you have someone working with you who has other circles of influence. Connie and I each did three parties a week for 15 years – and lived four blocks apart! We rarely crossed paths.

Expand your time

Connie was out working **at the same time** as me. It was almost like being two places at the same time!

I didn't know what I was doing when I recruited Connie. When I saw how happy it made **her**, I started to recruit on purpose. And that's when I learned another important lesson...

Not Every Recruit Is a Connie

Through the years, I recruited lots of people – and they didn't all go out and be tops in sales. Some of them didn't go out and do *anything*. But they all had the chance to. And that was the important thing. I could share the business opportunity with them and help them make a personal action plan to create their own success, but then the next step was theirs. They had to *choose* to do something with their business.

I don't believe that anyone starts with the intention of failing. But not everyone is willing to put in the effort that it takes to be successful. I spent way too many years struggling with this fact. I spent way too much energy trying to drag people across the finish line. Eventually, I realized that my responsibility was to provide the arena. *They* were the ones who had to show up and play!

Right about now, you are probably asking yourself, "Where do you find all these recruits?" This lesson is going to rock your world...

Prospects Are Everywhere

The world is full of people who may want what we have – an unlimited business opportunity that they can run from home. You already know some of the people; others you will meet; still others will be referred to you.

PEOPLE ON YOUR "WHO DO YOU KNOW?" LIST

When I am helping someone make an action plan to start her own home-based business, I encourage her to begin writing down the names of everyone she knows in a spiral notebook. This is the start of her "Who do you know?" list – a list that will continue to grow as long as she continues to build her business. I tell her not to prejudge who will be interested in one of her services...just write. She may not talk to them right away, but she will capture the names for later.

One day, I was doing a seminar. When we took a break, a lady approached me carrying a well-worn spiral notebook. She proudly showed me her "Who do you know?" list. It contained at least 20 pages of names and numbers. I congratulated her and flipped it open. I saw that the first page had many names with no notations.

I asked, "What happened when you talked to these people." She explained that she *hadn't* talked to them. She said she had written them down when she was new. She was afraid to call them because she thought she wouldn't know what to say. I said, "You're not new anymore. Would you like a challenge?" I challenged her to make her contacts that week from page one. I was delighted when I got her email a week later that said she had booked three parties and gotten two recruits from *page one of her list.*

A big "Who do you know?" list is like having a savings account with money tucked away for a rainy day. You *always* have someone to talk to. In Part 1 we talked about starting with your "C" names – the prospects you consider least likely to say, "Yes." However, I don't want you to ignore your family and close friends.

Keep in mind that the people you know best won't necessarily tell you what they need. They may have a hole in their life that your business opportunity can fill. You just don't know it. (*They* may not know it!) After all, why would you offer your wonderful business opportunity to strangers and ignore the people closest to you?

Another vast pool of prospects is…

PEOPLE YOU MEET WHEN YOU'RE OUT-AND-ABOUT

My friend Keith says, "It's a home-*based* business." Keith means that although you are based at home, many of your business-building activities take place away from home. That includes prospecting.

Get out. Meet people. See who needs one of your services. The more people you meet, the more you increase your odds of finding the people who are looking for you – they just don't know it yet!

Where do you go on a daily or weekly basis? Make a list of the places you go where you will meet people who might need your services...church, school, gym, bank, post office, etc.

If you made a very short list, here's a lesson I learned from my friend Ed...

"Circulate and cultivate"
If you always go to the same places, you're likely to see the same people. To meet new people, go different places. "Circulate and cultivate" is how Ed describes it. Go to a different place for coffee, try a new nail salon, take your clothes to a different dry cleaner, go to a different branch of your bank. We are all creatures of habit, so this may require a little stretching of your comfort zone. However, it's a sure way to meet new people to add to your "Who do you know?" list.

Go in...
Go into your bank. Go into the restaurant. Stop using the drive-through. Go into the post office instead of dropping your mail in a post box. When you go in, you meet people. When you meet people, you can strike up a conversation.

Dare yourself to do it!
My daughter, Katie, is very successful in sales. She shared with me that when she needs to do cold calls, she still gets nervous. She sits in her car and dares herself to go in. The dare gets her in the door. As soon as she's in, she feels a great sense of accomplishment, and that makes starting a conversation with the business-owner easier.

Become a "friend-finding" magnet

One of the best recruiters I ever met said, "I never go out to recruit. I go out to make friends. I am a friend-finding magnet." Pat smiles at people, pays them a compliment, asks them a question. He gets them talking. As they get comfortable talking to him, they begin to reveal what they need in their life – what's the hole in their life that his company is just waiting to fill. Don't go out to recruit. Go out to make friends.

A "fresh" spin on the 3-foot rule

You've probably heard of the 3-foot rule. It's usually defined as: "Anyone within three feet of you is someone to talk to about your product or business opportunity." Now **that** sounds pushy. It occurred to me that there is another spin you could put on the 3-foot rule. Think of it as "warming up the area three feet around you." Whether it's with a smile, a compliment, a comment or a question, you can find out who wants to talk to you and you *never* feel pushy.

Find the connection

Find out who **wants** to talk to you.

When I was growing up, there was a show on TV called *Watch Mr. Wizard*. Don Herbert, the creator, taught science to children in a fun, entertaining way. I was fascinated by every experiment he did, but my favorite was when Mr. Wizard constructed two towers to show how electricity works. When he flipped a switch and an arc of electricity jumped between the towers, it was like magic!

That's the magic connection you are looking for when you meet people. Smile at someone; pay a sincere compliment; make a comment; ask a question. See who responds. Sometimes when you smile at someone, or say, "Hello," the person may ignore you. Some people turn away. They may be shy or focused on whatever they are doing. They're not interested in talking to you, and *that's okay.*

Other people are hungry for contact with someone. The simplest way to make the magic happen is with a smile. Smile…even if you're in a hurry. A smile only takes an instant and it might make a big difference in somebody's day.

You can initiate conversation with a question, "Do you live around here?" "Know any good places to eat?" Or you can begin with a comment, "What a cute little girl!" or "I love your pin!" or "That's a great car!" You just want to see if they respond.

Don't be in a rush to bring up your business. Don't have an agenda to recruit somebody. Your only *agenda* is to build rapport and see if there's that little Mr. Wizard jump of electricity. When you feel that spark, you can exchange names and contact information. It's as simple as that!

Exchange contact information
My friend Ryane has the best technique I have ever heard for doing this. She simply hands the person she is talking to a card and says, "I've enjoyed talking with you. Here's my contact information…what's yours?" All one sentence – no pauses. She hands the person a little spiral notebook and a pen with her business card. It's a discreet

way of suggesting they write down their information in the little notebook.

Most people are anxious to exchange information. I have had people pull out a card. I have even had people pull a deposit slip out of their checkbook. If they give you their contact information, it's an invitation to call them. If they don't, don't worry about it. There are lots more people waiting to meet you.

PROSPECTS AT PARTIES

The biggest concentration of prospects is at your parties. Your hostess invited people from her circle of influence and those who said "Yes" were interested in something. They either liked her, they were interested in your product line, or they wanted to get out for an evening. So every hostess and every guest is a prospect.

Invite your hostess
Your hostess is your number one prospect. She likes you… she invited you into her home…she wants you to meet her friends. Invite *her* to find out more about doing what you do. You have five natural opportunities:

When you set the date for her party, say, "Many of our consultants were hostesses first, so I've included information about my business in your hostess packet. If you have any questions, don't hesitate to ask me."

When you follow up on the phone, ask, "Is there anything about what I do that looks good to you?"

When you get to her home, inquire, "On a scale of 1 to 10 with 10 being, 'How soon can I get started?' – where are you?"

When you use your Survey Slip, ask the guests to indicate whether they would book a party if the hostess decided to start her own business.

When you close her party, remind her the business opportunity is still available. Let her know you'd be happy to help her get started.

Invite every guest

If you don't invite *everyone,* you may miss *someone* who needs what you have to offer. My friend Tina has had a successful career in party plan for 20 years. However, she may never have gotten started if she hadn't gone to three parties. Here's what happened:

Tina went to her first home party when her son was just a few months old. She was a school teacher and didn't have a lot of money to spend, but when the consultant offered Tina the opportunity to purchase educational books for her son, she purchased.

At the next home party Tina attended, the consultant described two services: the chance to purchase and the chance to get free products by booking a party. Tina purchased and booked.

At the third party Tina attended, the consultant said, "I care very much about serving the needs of all of my customers." After reviewing her first two services, she said, "For

124

"How May I Serve You?"

Name _____ Date_____

Address _____

City / State _____Zip_____

Email for Specials _____

Best Phone # to reach me:_____

Best time to reach me:_____

I am interested in:

Information about the business opportunity:

❑   Not at the moment

❑   I might consider it

❑   Let's talk!

Getting my friends together for a party:

❑   No, thanks

❑   Hmm…maybe

❑   Let's pick a date!

❑   If our hostess starts her own business, count me in!

Being informed when you have specials:
❑   No, thanks

❑   Absolutely!

those who could use some extra money or who have considered starting your own business, I invite you to watch what I do tonight and talk with me later." The consultants at the first two parties hadn't mentioned an income opportunity. When the third consultant shared this service, Tina realized that her dream of being home with her infant son could become a reality. What a shame that Tina had to wait so long for someone to invite her!

Chocolate chip cookies

Imagine that you are having a party and you baked a batch of delicious chocolate chip cookies. They are still warm when the first guest arrives. You offer her a cookie and she says, "No, thank you." Will you offer a cookie to the next guest...and the next...and the next? Or will you put the cookies away in the kitchen because someone didn't want a cookie? Can you tell by looking who will want a cookie? Even if you know that one of your guests has been on Weight Watchers and is being really careful, you will still offer her a cookie. Who knows...she may have been saving up her points all day because she loves your chocolate chip cookies!

People are never offended when you offer. However, they may be offended if you *don't* offer.

A fourth endless pool of prospects is...

REFERRALS

When I started my business, one of my personal friends was already very successful in his own business. Bob Mayberry owned a thriving insurance agency. He sat down with me and shared some valuable tips. One of the most important things he taught me was the importance of referrals. Bob said, "Most of your new business will come from referrals from satisfied customers. A referral is a 'warm contact' because someone she trusts, trusts you."

Bob also taught me that you have to ask for referrals. Simply say, "The greatest compliment you can pay me is to refer me to your friends." Offer a referral sheet and suggest she write down a few names right away. Most people have their friends' names and telephone numbers stored in their cell phone, so it is simple for them to fill out the form while they're talking to you.

Referral Information

The greatest compliment you can pay me is to refer me to your friends! Please take a minute and tell me about people you think may be interested in any of my services:

- Purchasing product
- Having a party
- Joining my team

Name	Phone #	Relationship
1.		
2.		
3.		
4.		
5.		

© A Fresh Perspective, Inc.   www.getafreshperspective.com   Phone: 401.247.0556
Lyn Conway   lyn@getafreshperspective.com   Fax: 401.247.4834

The Fortune Is in the Follow-Up

Years ago, I read an amazing statistic on the website for the National Sales Executive Association. The statistics illustrate the average number of contacts that are made with people who *eventually* say, "Yes" to a product or service.

Look at this:

2% of sales are made on the first contact.

3% of sales are made on the second contact.

5% of sales are made on the third contact.

10% of sales are made on the fourth contact.

Through the fourth contact, only 20% of the people who are going to say, "Yes," have said "Yes."

80% of sales are made on the 5th through 12th contact!

These statistics are not just for the direct sales industry. These are for the sale of every product or service. In fact, they hold true for everything. It takes most of us awhile to get used to an idea.

Think about it. You see a product advertised on television and say, "That's a good idea!" You may even write down the phone number or address, but you probably don't take action right away. It's not *that* important to you yet. After you see that product advertised a few more times, you are finally ready to take action.

The temptation is to quit after three or four contacts if your prospect hasn't said, "Yes." We don't want to feel "pushy." Look at the statistics. You double the results on the fourth contact and the real payoff is on the 5th through 12th contact. Plus, if you quit after contacting the person four times, the next person who talks to your prospect has an 80% better chance because you gave up!

Everyone Has a Story

Tell yours. People join people not companies. When people get to know you…like you…trust you, they are much more likely to want to join your team.

When you write your WHY story, include these points:

- What you were doing when you found your company?
- Why did you decide to get started?
- Why is your life better because you did?
- Why do you recommend your company to others?

Keep it short – no more than one page – and photocopy it on pretty paper. Include it with everything you hand out: catalogs, hostess packets, opportunity packets. Everything!

You Never Know When You Are With Your Next Recruit

You never know who is going to be touched by your story. You never know who joins you because she feels a kinship with you. Your recruit is usually watching you long before you sign her up. She may be a friend, a hostess or a party guest. She is watching and listening to you. Often, you are the only model of a "successful home-based business person" that she has.

My WHY Story

_____

_____

_____

_____

_____

_____

_____

_____

_____

_____

_____

_____

_____

_____

When you have a consistent, successful business, you are more likely to recruit people who duplicate your *actions* and your *attitudes*. But here's a little hint…

STOP LOOKING FOR YOURSELF

Successful people often tell me they want to recruit someone just like them. They would have missed me. I was nothing like I am now when Lenore met me.

> ***Stop looking for a finished product and start looking for "raw material."***

You can't tell by looking who will be interested in your business. And you can't tell by looking who will develop into a rock star! Stop looking for a finished product and start looking for "raw material." They will look to you as a role-model, but they won't all be willing to do what it takes to be successful. That was probably the hardest lesson I ever learned…

Don't Want It More for Them Than They Want It for Themselves

This one is such a hard lesson to learn. When I signed someone up, I wanted her to be successful. I felt responsible.

Prospect Follow-up Log   Month _____ Year _____

NAME, PHONE, E-MAIL	1ST CONTACT (when, where)	NOTES	FOLLOW-UP DATES

© A Fresh Perspective, Inc.   www.getafreshperspective.com   Phone: 401.247.0556
Lyn Conway   lyn@getafreshperspective.com   Fax: 401.247.4834

However, I discovered that I often wanted it more for my recruit than she wanted it for herself. I would think, "She could be so good." Or, "She needs the money so much." I would try to drag my recruits along. I finally realized that dragging people sapped both my time and my energy.

The sooner you learn this lesson, the happier you will be: you can't take credit for someone else's success and you are not responsible for their failure. You are responsible for telling her the truth about your company as you know it and for illustrating the actions that lead to success. But you can't do it *for* your recruits. No one has that much stamina.

The recruits who do follow your lead – who are persistent and consistent in their efforts – have the opportunity to learn all the lessons you have learned!

PART 5

Universal Lessons

Universal Lessons

There is an old expression in Missouri, the "Show-Me" state: "I'll believe it when I see it." My favorite expression is the exact opposite: "I'll *see it* when I *believe it.*" I *don't* believe in coincidence. A lot of amazing things have happened to me, but I don't think they were coincidences. I believe I attracted them. When you visualize the life that you want, all the powers in the universe conspire to help you create it. This is one of the greatest universal lessons of all...

"I'll See It When I Believe It!"

Some people tell me, "I don't really know what I want." Don't worry – most people aren't used to visualizing the life they would *really* like to live. We can fix that! You will need a couple of tools and about 30 minutes.

Here's what you need:
> ➤ Two or three of your favorite magazines that you're willing to cut up
> ➤ Scissors or an exacto knife
> ➤ Glue stick or tape
> ➤ Poster board or a large sheet of paper

Here's what you do:

Flip through the magazines, don't read – just flip. Give yourself about 15 minutes, and see what jumps out at you. Pictures…phrases…words…your subconscious mind will select them. Cut them out, then attach them to a poster board or large piece of paper to make a collage. Hang the collage where you will see it every day. You will be amazed at how this little activity helps you clarify what you want in your life.

Posting pictures has astonishing power. Let me tell you a story…

THE POWER OF PICTURES

Dan and I both grew up spending our summers at lake cottages. Both of our families had boats. Dan had a speedboat when I married him and we spent a lot of our leisure time boating. Then we had kids. Speedboat, water-skiing, babies – they didn't mix so we sold the boat. As the kids got bigger, we missed boating so we said, "Let's get another boat!"

We spent one long, cold Chicago winter looking through boating magazines. We cut out a picture of the boat that we both liked – a 19-foot Celebrity Bow-Rider, silver gray with a burgundy stripe – and put it on the refrigerator. Well, I don't know about your refrigerator, but ours was cluttered with pictures the kids drew at school, coupons and shopping lists, receipts, schedules… The picture of the boat blended in and we didn't even see it after awhile.

In late May, we said, "It's time to buy our boat!" We had decided to buy a used boat, so we started each day by reading the classified ads. We called about the ones that sounded interesting. We looked at a few that were absolutely *not* "the boat." One had possibilities…it was being sold by an older couple who were buying a bigger boat. It sounded like the boat had been well-cared for, so we went to see it. We both liked it and the price was right. We said, "We'll take it."

We drove home with the boat and pulled it into the alley behind our house. I went in to crack a couple of cold ones to celebrate our new boat. As I opened the refrigerator door, I  spotted the picture of the boat that we had put up there months before. I went out to the alley and I said, "Dan, you're not going to believe this. We bought the boat that's on the refrigerator!" We didn't buy a similar boat; we bought the boat that was in the picture – a 19-foot Celebrity Bow-rider, silver gray with a burgundy stripe. And it was a used boat that we found in the classified ads!

Sounds like an amazing coincidence, doesn't it? I don't believe that for a moment! It's not coincidence or magic. It's electromagnetic energy. You project out to the world what you want, and the world responds by sending you what you ask for.

We named that boat "The Silver Fox" after my husband (who has beautiful silver hair). When we moved first to California and then to Rhode Island, the boat moved with us.

After we had been in Rhode Island for a couple of years and I was working in another corporate position, I started to think to myself, "I'm not really very happy working in a corporate environment. (It was about that time that the title of this book came to me.) I really wanted my own business again, but I was afraid to make the leap.

Take a Leap

I was asked to speak at a Direct Selling Association meeting in June. DSA is the national trade association for firms in the direct sales industry and my topic was recruiting. I was nervous presenting to so many high-powered executives, so I asked my friends to sit in the front row to encourage me.

One of the people whose support I enlisted was Marcia Wieder. Marcia is a well-known speaker and author of the best-selling book *Making Your Dreams Come True*. She came up to me after my presentation and said, "You were really good!" I said, "Thank you. Don't sound so surprised!" And she said, "You know, you could do that professionally." I responded, "I thought I just did!" Marcia went on to explain that she meant I could be a professional speaker like her. She asked, "Have you ever thought about it?" I told her I had thought about it and went on to tell her why I couldn't do it – just as anyone does when she is afraid to take a risk or do something new. Marcia was very gracious. I'm sure she knew I was making excuses, but she continued, "Well, I'll tell you what. When you get ready, call me and I'll help you get started."

A few weeks after she planted that seed, I decided to contact Marcia and find out what I needed to do to go out on my own. I called her and she was wonderful. She helped me make an action plan for starting my business, and at the end of the conversation, she made a suggestion. She said, "I want you to write a page in the 'book of your life.'" I asked her what she meant, and she told me that the "book of your life" is where you write down how you see your future. "Write *in the present tense* – as if it had already happened. Don't write, 'I want to exercise.' Instead write, 'I exercise four days a week and I'm in great shape.' Instead of writing, 'I want to buy a convertible,' change it to, 'I love riding around in my convertible with the top down.'"

So I did it. Five or six days later, I got up very early. I sat at the kitchen table. The thoughts had been percolating in my mind. I wrote everything on a single piece of notebook paper. I wrote it in the present tense. I included details about every area of my life, including starting my own business. Through an amazing set of circumstances (not coincidences!), I was able to start A Fresh Perspective, Inc. just two months later. One year later, when I looked back at the page I had written, every single thing on the page had happened…with only one exception. I had written down that I was living in a house on the water, and I wasn't there yet.

I was teaching a seminar a few months later and told this story. My husband had accompanied me and was sitting in the back of the room. When I got to the part about the house on the water, Dan commented, "I want a bigger boat. *She* wants the house on the water." Someone in the audience said, "Well the big boat could *be* the house on the water." Dan and I looked at each other and we said, "It really *could*!"

Once again, we started looking through boating magazines. We decided that we wanted a single-engine, 30-foot trawler; however, all the used boats we would have liked to look at were on the West Coast. A month later, Dan called me and said, "There is a trawler for sale 30 minutes from our house. The ad is in the classified section of the Providence Journal. It sounds like what we're looking for." I said, "Go see it!" He called me from the dock and said, "I think you should come over here." Dan met me in the parking lot and began describing the features of the boat. I spotted it as we

 walked up the dock and said, "We're buying that boat." Dan said, "You haven't been *on* the boat yet. You don't even know if it *runs*." I said, "That's our boat. We visualized it and here it is."

When you visualize your success…see your life as you want it to be…the image you create in your mind becomes your reality. Your conscious mind only knows what you tell it, so you have to dare to imagine the life you want. Take a leap! Invent your life in your mind first, put it on paper, and be prepared for things to start to happen.

What do you want? Write it in the "book of your life." Give it rich detail. You will see it when you believe it. You will attract it to yourself just like a magnet. You will also attract people like a magnet. People love to be with someone who is positive and enthusiastic. This cosmic lesson has amazing implications for your business and your life…

It's All About the Relationships

There is a common misconception that your income from your home-based direct sales business is a result of how much you sell and recruit. In fact, the money you earn is actually a reflection of how many relationships you have developed and how strong those relationships are. I had a dramatic lesson in this in February, 1987...

One of my mottos is, "As January goes, so goes the year." My team and I had had an outstanding January. We had all worked very hard. I had decided that I was going to take some time off, so I had booked very few parties for February. The company that I was with at the time never notified us about contests and incentives in advance. We were notified by mail the first day of the new month. (I still have never figured out how they got the US Postal Service to cooperate in getting the mail to us on time. How different things are now in the electronic age!)

It was the last day of January and the president of the company came to Chicago to attend a meeting we were holding. He took Lucia and me out to lunch after the meeting. At lunch, he told us that he would give us a "sneak preview" of the February contest. He pulled a full-color brochure out of his briefcase. It had a picture of Ireland on the front. I scanned it briefly and saw that it was a contest with lots of beautiful "Irish" prizes – things like Waterford crystal. Then I looked at the top prize – an all-expense paid trip for two to Ireland. There would only be one winner – the person with the highest personal sales in February.

I was *furious*. I was usually the top salesperson, but I had planned to work very little in February. I said to the president of the company, "You knew I planned to take some time off! You know that Dan Conway is Irish and has never been to Ireland! This isn't fair!" He just grinned sheepishly. I left that lunch and had a decision to make. I decided that I had to go for it, even though I was starting with a virtually empty booking calendar. I was going to take my Irishman to Ireland.

"I Need Your Help"

When I got home, I pulled out my entire contact log and started making phone calls. I called past hostesses and guests and said, "I need your help." I explained my goal and asked if they would have a home party or gather enough orders for a catalog party. I filled my February calendar with bookings for home shows and set dates to close catalog parties. Help came from everywhere.

Toward the end of the month, I got several phone calls from people I hardly knew offering to place an order. They said things like, "Tricia told me you need help," or "I heard you have a big goal. How are you doing?" The problem was that I had no way to know. I didn't need a certain *amount* of sales. I needed to be #1 in personal sales for the month of February. I was astonished at the outpouring of support. And I *did* take Dan to Ireland on that trip, thanks to all the people who cared about me and my goal.

One of my most treasured memories is being at Knappogue Castle in County Clare, Ireland on a glorious June evening. Dan and I were crowned "the Earl and his Lady" and piped into the castle for a sumptuous banquet...all thanks to the relationships I had built with hostesses and customers. I was very grateful to all of them.

Learning to approach life with an attitude of gratitude is one of the most wonderful lessons I have ever learned...

An Attitude of Gratitude

"The last of the human freedoms
is to choose one's attitude."
~Victor Frankl

When I started to have trouble with my hips, I didn't think it was a big deal. I was sad to give up jogging, but I found other forms of exercise that I liked and *could* do. Over the course of a few short years, the problem got much worse. I started to visit orthopedic surgeons. They told me that I had degenerative arthritis in my hips, but that I was *too young* for hip replacements. Eventually, I could hardly walk. I finally convinced one surgeon to do the surgery. My argument was that I might be only 55 years old, but I felt 85 years old and couldn't stand being incapacitated when there was a solution available. We scheduled a conventional hip-replacement surgery for July 27th. The recovery time would be about three months.

That Easter, my friend Lucia sent me a card with a clipping from the Chicago Tribune. It described a new, experimental hip-replacement surgery – a minimally invasive surgery with a much shorter hospital stay and a *much* shorter recovery time. Her note said, "I hate to even bring this up because I know you're already scheduled, but I thought you might want to investigate this."

On Easter Sunday, 2004, Dan and I sat at the computer and researched the new procedure. No one in Rhode Island was doing it, but there were two doctors in Boston who were pioneering it in the Northeast. The internet articles described the kind of candidates the doctors were looking for.

I got on the telephone on Monday morning. The first person who answered was the lady who scheduled patients for Dr. Rubash, the head of Orthopedic Surgery at Massachusetts General Hospital in Boston. I said, "I am the perfect candidate for Dr. Rubash. I'm not too old. I don't have too much body fat. My general health is excellent and I have a good attitude. I want Dr. Rubash to replace my hip this summer." She laughed and said, "Why don't we make an appointment for a consultation and we'll let the doctor decide about that."

Dr. Rubash replaced my first hip August 24th and my second hip the following March 8th. I was out of the hospital within 24 hours each time and walking without crutches within a week of each surgery. I am so grateful to live at a time when these kinds of miracles are possible.

My old hips were made of bone. My new hips are made of metal. So, every time I go through airport security, I set off the alarm. As I approach, I tell them, "New hips. I'm going to set off the alarm." The routine is about the same every time: they put me in a little holding pen until a lady with a wand approaches. I hold up one leg, then the other. I stand with my arms out – palms up – and she scans me and we chat and have a good time. For me, it's a matter of choosing my attitude. I could get really bent out of shape that I have to do this EVERY time I go through security. But, it's a fact of life. I choose to make a good moment out of it. On one of my recent trips, the lady who scanned me said, "You're good to go…and thank you for being a bright spot in my day."

Choose an attitude of gratitude and you will find bright spots in every day!

Find a Coach

When you have your own home-based business, you have to be more disciplined and determined than you would if you worked for someone else. You don't have anyone to tell you *what* to do and *when* to do it. You are the boss. Everyone who works from home finds herself getting discouraged or getting off course at one time or another. For that reason, I recommend that you find a coach who can help you stay on track.

My husband was actually my first coach, although neither of us knew it at the time. He asked me good questions to help me identify what was working and what I needed to tweak. He gave me a push or threw me a lifeline when I got really discouraged. I remember one of those moments distinctly…

I was standing at the kitchen sink washing dishes with the phone wedged between my ear and my shoulder. Dan was at his office listening to me cry about how overwhelmed I was feeling. He asked, "When's the last time you worked out at the gym?" I really couldn't remember. He said, "Go to the gym." I did. Of course, I began to feel better almost immediately.

There are really two lessons here:

- The first lesson is that you need someone you trust and respect to coach you. It may be a friend, relative or business acquaintance, but there is someone out there. Find that person so you won't feel like you have to go it alone.

- The second lesson is that you must find a way to fill your tank when you start to feel tired or discouraged.

Take Time for "Re-creation"

> "People who cannot find time for recreation are obliged sooner of later to find time for illness."
> ~John Wanamaker

What helps you fill your tank? Do you like to read... exercise...go to a movie...sit in the sunshine...go out to lunch? Whatever it is, schedule time to restore your spirit. Recreation isn't a luxury – it's a necessity. If you don't take time to re-create, you will deplete your energy reserves and risk "burn-out." I always feel sad when someone tells me that she is going to quit because she is "burned out." In reality, the problem is usually just bad balance between work and play. If you start to feel this way, take some time for yourself – some time for re-creation. It's not selfish – it's essential for having the energy that you need to run a successful business.

Also essential is surrounding yourself with supportive people…

The Company You Keep

"Listening is a magnetic and strange thing, a creative force. The friends who listen to us are the ones we move toward. When we are listened to, it creates us, makes us unfold and expand."
~Karl Menninger

I heard an interesting statistic: your income will be the average of the income of your five closest friends. At first I was skeptical; then I thought of my own situation. My closest friends were other successful women who owned their own business. Dan's and my closest friends were all very successful people. Some were business owners; some were corporate executives or educators – all were successful. It makes sense. Your closest friends provide a reflection of what's possible.

Many years ago, Dan and I visited our dear friends Pat and Dick Wakenight. We had met through Marriage Encounter early in my career, so they had watched my growth through the years. Dick was a very successful executive for a large corporation and had offered impromptu coaching whenever he thought it would help me.

Pat and Dick had moved out-of-state, so we were visiting for the weekend. As we sat talking at their kitchen table, Dick asked me, "Where do you see yourself in ten years?" I thought for a moment and responded, "I'd like to be a professional speaker." Without hesitating, he said, "Then that is what you'll do." I have to admit that I had never considered being a speaker until he asked the question. It had just popped into my mind, but afterwards, it seemed the most natural thing in the world.

Pay attention to the people with whom you spend the most time. Choose people who challenge you...people who encourage you and believe in you. Steer clear of "dream stealers" – people who are jealous of you and your success...people who talk to you about what's *not* possible. In so many ways, you *are* the company you keep.

"A friend hears the song
in my heart and sings it to me
when my memory fails."
~Anonymous

Daddy's Not a Babysitter

You may have people ask, "Does your husband babysit when you do your parties?" The best answer I ever heard to this question came from a lady who ran a successful home-based business and did parties regularly. She told me, "I always respond, 'Babysit? Of course not...we have five children of our own.'" She gave me permission to share that with you...it stops them cold!

One of the most wonderful blessings that we experienced because I went out to do parties was the relationship Dan developed with Danny and Katie. When he wasn't in school on Tuesday and Thursday night, he got the kids all to himself. He played with them and read them bedtime stories. He knew how to change diapers and get their temperature to come down if one of them ran a fever. If they fell down, they were as likely to call "Daddy!" as "Mommy!" They are both adults now and still have an incredible relationship with their father.

And now, it's time for one final, universal lesson...

You Are Here

I learned this lesson from an eight-year old. I hope you will remember it anytime you feel discouraged or inadequate.

Lucia and I were attending a National Conference being held in a large hotel complex. Our husbands and children were with us. They were enjoying the indoor pool, watching movies and playing video games while we were in meetings. At the mid-morning break, Lucia and I checked in with the men and saw that Joey, Lucia's youngest son, was missing. We were concerned, but the guys said, "Go back to your meetings. We've got it under control." At lunch, Joey was still missing. Once again, the men told us not to worry. They had it covered.

When we returned mid-afternoon, Joey was happily watching TV. We hugged him and told him that we had been worried about him. He looked away from the television with a puzzled expression, so we continued, "You were lost for a long time." Joey responded, "I was never lost. Everywhere I went, there was a map on the wall that said, 'You are here.'" If you start to feel lost, remember Joey. You are here and there is always a map available to help you get where you want to go.

"I Hope You Dance"

A few years ago, I was flipping stations on my car radio as I was driving. I caught the last minute of a song that brought me to tears because it was so beautiful. I called my kids and said, "I just heard this beautiful song about dancing. Do you know what it is?" Of course, they thought I was nuts – there are only a million or so songs about dancing.

A month later, Dan and I sat in church on Mother's Day. The priest saying the mass said he had a special treat for all the mothers in church that morning. He had arranged for a woman who sang professionally to sing a song for us that Lee Ann Womack had recorded for her daughter. As she began to sing, I realized that it was the "dancing song" that I had heard on the radio. I think of each of you as my daughter, even though I may never have met you. I wish you great success in your business. I hope you live out your most wonderful dreams, and I hope you dance!

"I Hope You Dance"

I hope you never lose your sense of wonder
You get your fill to eat
But always keep that hunger
May you never take one single breath for granted
God forbid love ever leave you empty handed
I hope you still feel small
When you stand by the ocean
Whenever one door closes, I hope one more opens
Promise me you'll give faith a fighting chance

And when you get the choice to sit it out or dance
I hope you dance

I hope you never fear those mountains in the distance
Never settle for the path of least resistance
Living might mean taking chances
But they're worth taking
Lovin' might be a mistake
But it's worth making
Don't let some hell bent heart
Leave you bitter
When you come close to selling out
Reconsider
Give the heavens above
More than just a passing glance

And when you get the choice to sit it out or dance
I hope you dance

About the Author

 Lyn Conway is a professional speaker/trainer/author with more than 30 years experience in the direct sales profession. Lyn offers a unique three-dimensional perspective: she achieved exceptional success as a top seller, recruiter and field leader, as a corporate executive and as the owner of her own company. Having learned lessons about working from home in each of those situations, she is dedicated to sharing what she's learned with you.

Lyn is recognized as a role-model for entrepreneurs. She teaches and trains with confidence and passion. Her seminars and keynote presentations blend sound theory and practical experience with humor so that her listeners leave ready to take action. Her audience knows that she has "walked the talk."

Lyn started *A Fresh Perspective, Inc.* in 1997 to help entrepreneurs reach their full potential. Her mission is to help *you* achieve *your own vision of success*. She knows that it is not easy to do what it takes to be successful in your own business. She also knows, from personal experience, that the rewards are enormous when you do! Fun, friendship, self-confidence and financial security – they are all within your reach.

Contact Lyn by telephone or email:
Telephone – 877.441.6782
Email – lyn@getafreshperspective.com

Also by Lyn Conway

SEMINARS AND KEYNOTE PRESENTATIONS

Success Seminars: Customized seminars with instant take-away have an immediate impact on the growth of your business. Lyn establishes rapport with the audience and encourages participation throughout. These seminars are a blend of sound theory, practical experience and techniques to take home and use today!

Keynote Presentations: When Lyn speaks, it's from experience and her audience knows it. Lyn's message touches both the mind and the heart. Listeners leave prepared to take action!

Lyn knows how important it is to choose the right speaker for your event. She works with you every step of the way to make your event perfect.

View snippets of some of Lyn's presentations on her website: www.getafreshperspective.com

AUDIO/CD PROGRAMS

Language of Success
Six hours of basic training for every skill level
This series includes:
CD 1 – Self-Talk
CD 2 – "Ring Up" Rewards
CD 3 – Bookings Mean Business
CD 4 – Relationship Recruiting
CD 5 – The Success Wheel

Contact with Confidence
Two hours of training for every skill level
CD 1 – Prospect and Follow-up with Confidence
CD 2 – Address Concerns, Hesitations and Objections

Love 'em & Lead 'em
Six hours of Leadership Training
This series includes:
CD 1 – Live the Dream
CD 2 – Your Leadership Journey
CD 3 – Keys to Coaching
CD 4 – Coaching Conversations
CD 5 – Target Your Success

QUAD Coaching
Two hours of advanced training on coaching
CD 1 – Coaching with the QUAD
CD 2 – QUAD Coaching in Action

New products are being released all the time.
To find out what's new, please visit our website.
www.getafreshperspective.com

TELE-COURSES

Please visit Lyn's website for a complete list of courses.
www.getafreshperspective.com

Order Information

Quantity	Item Ordered	Price Per Item	Total
	Makeup Optional (Book)	$14.95	$
	Makeup Optional (Audio) (2 CD set)	$27.95	$
	Value Pack – Book & Audio	$35.95	$
	Other		$
	Shipping & Handling (All orders shipped Priority Mail) US orders – $5.50 for the first book or audio. $0.75 for each additional item	$5.50 + _____	
	Canadian orders – $9.00 for the first book or audio. $0.75 for each additional item	$9.00 + _____	
			$_____

Order Total $ _____

Check enclosed for $_____ (payable to *A Fresh Perspective, Inc.*)

Charge my ❑ Visa ❑ MasterCard ❑ Discover

Account # _____

Expiration Date _____   3-digit Security Code _____

Print Name _____

Signature _____

Address _____

_____

Telephone Number (_____) _____

Mail to: Lyn Conway   Fax orders to:
A Fresh Perspective, Inc.   401.247.4834
47 Asylum Road   Phone orders to:
Warren, RI 02885   877.441.6782

You may also place a secure order online at www.getafreshperspective.com
Questions? Please call toll-free or email: lyn@getafreshperspective.com